The GardenWay Bread Book

The GardenWay
Bread Book

A BAKER'S ALMANAC

ELLEN FOSCUE JOHNSON

GARDEN WAY PUBLISHING
CHARLOTTE, VERMONT 05445

ACKNOWLEDGMENT

This book was made by many people. We would like to thank all those who shared their time, recipes, experiences in baking, and gave of themselves for photographs:

Nancy Adelman, Mary Ballou, Sarah, Jennifer and Tamasin Ballou, Debbie Beckwith, Billy Beckwith, Posy Benedict, Elizabeth Bowden, Mary Frances Byrne, Heman and Edith Chase, Kendra Cheney, Barbara Comfort, Cortlandt Creech, Nancy Cortner, Lisman Cortner, Nancy Dalley, Mary Decker, David Decker, Frank Doran, Diane Dunnigan, Jeremy Dworkin, Rachel Dworkin, Tom Ettinger, Jewell Everhart, Valworth Foscue, Joan Fox, James, Sarah and Alexander Fox, Gigi Gamper, Dorothy Hard, Leo Heer, Laura Heller, Gail and Ed Holden, Scott Howell, Walt Hudgins, Christopher Johnson, Janet Langdon, Fay LaPrade, Carole Lechthaler, Virginia Lezhnev, Nancy Livermore, Penny Lowe, Susie MacDonald, Tony and Jackie Marro, Jim Marro, Florence McCreary, John McLure, Kay Moss, Margaret Newton, Sandy and Wendy Noyes, Sam and Sheila Ogden, Sally Ogden, Lyman Orton, Inge Parnas, Charles Parnell, Mary Partridge, Cora Partridge, Martha Punderson, Linda Punderson, Sam Punderson, Grace Reitzel, Nancy Rice, Martha Salomon, Irene Smith, Arnold Steinhardt, Louise Stevenson, Aggie Sullivan, Mary Sweeney, Donald R. Taylor, Virginia Johnson Taylor, Mary Thompson, Barbara Tozier, Barbara Trask, Joan Wagner, Tony Western, Virginia Wilson, Doug Williams, Philip Zimmerman.

Also, the Bakery at Old Salem, N.C.; Baile's Old Mill, Oak Ridge, N.C.; Falls Mill, Belvidere, Tenn.; The Old Grist Mill, Weston, Vt.; Schoolhouse Farm, Warren, Me.; Tryon Palace Commission, New Bern, N.C.; The Vermont Country Store, Rockingham, Vt.

Photographs by Ellen Foscue Johnson
Cover, interior design and illustrations by Trezzo/Braren Studio
Third Printing, October 1979
Library of Congress Cataloging in Publication Data

Johnson, Ellen Foscue.
  The Garden Way bread book.

  Includes index.
  1. Bread. I. Title.
TX769.J62   641.8′15   79-46-2
ISBN 0-88266-140-X
ISBN 0-88266-139-6 pbk.

Contents

Contents

Introduction

In The Beginning: Love and Nutrition

You—man, woman, or child—can make your own bread. A well-equipped kitchen, a leisurely schedule, and a sophisticated market will allow you to explore the refinements of this encyclopedic craft. But **none** of these is necessary. Breadmaking is an activity which, even at its humblest, is creative, impressive, and useful.

If you have a bag of flour, a source of water, a store where you can buy some yeast (even that you can "grow" or do without) and access to a stove, or failing that a fireplace or an outdoor fire, you can make the kind of bread that has sustained the human race for several thousand years. And some of the classic breads are the simplest.

But isn't there more to it than that? Yes, but the rest is in the doing, which is what this book is about. And you can do it.

One thing this country needs, more than a chicken in every pot, is a loaf (with substance) on every hearth. A misconception of our times is that bread is only a starch, something you serve in the place of white rice, and the first thing to cut out when you go on a diet. Far from it. Almost from the beginning bread has been a vital constituent of human nutrition. Certainly this is true of Western civilization, the civilization which generated so many great and life-sustaining breads and in due course developed the technology to render that bread expendable.

Recently a child visitor to our house rejected a peanut butter and jelly sandwich because it was presented on homemade bread, not the store-bought kind he was used to. Children do become addicted to what they are raised on and, just as we are told many American children now prefer frozen or canned orange juice to fresh, real bread may turn them off at first. Many adults can remember something better, but to those who can't and to many children, the richness, crunchiness, chewiness and subtle flavors of homemade bread make demands on their palates and jaw muscles, whereas the flaccid white stuff from the store can be consumed in one fell chomp. Convenience food for convenience chewing.

Everyone has noticed the recent efforts of bread companies to cater to a renewed interest in more healthful, whole-grain food. This is commendable as far as it goes, but it doesn't go very far. These breads still cannot hold a candle to the ones you make yourself. The whole-grain effect is often an illusion produced by coloring. Even "all-natural" loaves may not have a great deal of substance. The teeth test will tell you, as will the label. Even if your heart's desire is plain white bread, the loaf you make will be honest and beautiful from the inside out. Once you start making bread you may never buy another commercial loaf. Does that sound like too much of a commitment? It does make some demands on your energy and time, but they are well worth the giving.

A choice of yeasts.

Why Make Bread?

Because . . .

it is a skill that will give you a feeling of accomplishment when you have mastered it.

it is an art form of universal appeal, historical significance and inexhaustible variety.

it is a little different every time, therefore its interest, and even suspense, are never diminished.

it involves an inherent tension between the scientific and the subjective.

you never learn everything there is to know.

it embraces the primitive and the rarified.

it will add pleasure to your life and to the lives of those who break bread with you.

and in addition to all this, it is good for you!

This is a book by a student for other students. Just as I have learned something every day in the process of putting this book together, I expect to continue learning for the rest of my life—and so will you. Baking bread is a lifetime adventure. May you pursue and rejoice in it.

Necessities

1. Yeast or some other leavener (usually)
2. Water
3. Flour
4. Bowl or other container
5. Wooden or similar strong spoon
6. Two knives and a fork (for some kinds of mixing)
7. Surface for kneading
8. Something to bake on or in (pan, cookie sheet, tile, coffee can)
9. Something to cover dough (towel, shirt, pillowcase)
10. Oven (stove top, fireplace or outdoor fire)

Nice Things to Work With

1. Salt
2. Milk
3. Eggs
4. Butter and oil
5. Nutritional additives
6. Several kinds of flours
7. Several kinds of sweeteners
8. Measuring cup
9. Measuring spoons
10. Two bowls
11. Electric mixer or hand beater
12. Loaf pans
13. Sharp knife
14. Rubber spatula
15. Single-edged razor for slashing loaves
16. Pancake turner
17. Pastry scraper
18. Pastry brush
19. Wire rack
20. Reliable oven and/or good oven thermometer
21. Thermometer for measuring temperature of water
22. Wire whisk
23. Pastry blender

Options and frills

Fruits, nuts, seeds

A variety of flours and meals

Occasionally, liquors and liqueurs

Two pastry brushes, one for melted butter, one for glazes.

Different sizes of bread pans, a variety of casseroles, souffle dishes, tube pan, fluted molds, special French bread pan.

A large convenient surface which is used only for kneading bread

Heavy duty electric mixer with dough hook

Plant mister for spraying

THE BASIC LOAF

LAURA'S EASY, BASIC AND GOOD WHITE BREAD

First assemble all your ingredients within reaching distance.

1 tablespoon dry yeast
2 cups warm water
2 tablespoons honey
2 tablespoons light oil
2 teaspoons salt
5 to 6 cups unbleached white flour
2 tablespoons raw wheat germ
½ cup non-fat dry milk

Making bread is not difficult. Like other activities which we soon enough take for granted (driving a car, planting a garden), there are a number of steps which must be linked together in sequence. But that sequence is flexible in its tempo. There are few dogmas in baking, few exacting moments, few measurements which must be precise. Making bread intimidates people because the behavior of yeast mystifies them (they don't quite trust it) and the number of steps seems oppressively large and complex. But after you have done it a few times, you will assimilate this seeming complexity into the pattern of your life until you can make bread with a light heart, confidence and, finally, abandon.

Let's take one good, simple bread from start to finish, elaborating each step so as to banish awe. These instructions are given in tedious detail; stripped of words, this is a simple procedure. *The sequence and methods are to be applied to every yeast bread in this book.* Once you understand them—by reading—the whole process can be reduced to a paragraph. Once you understand them—by doing—you can bake anything.

Equipment

measuring spoons
measuring cup
thermometer if available
large mixing bowl (one which goes with an electric mixer if you have one)
large wooden spoon
another large bowl (for rising dough)
two loaf pans or a baking sheet
wire rack

If you don't have honey, use sugar.

If you don't have the oil, use melted butter or margarine.

If you don't have wheat germ, leave it out.

If you don't have dry milk, use one cup whole or skim milk in place of one cup of the water.

If you don't have unbleached white flour, use bleached, but know that your bread will taste and be better after you have gotten some unbleached. Or use whole wheat and increase the yeast to 1½ tablespoons.

If you don't have yeast, maybe you'd better wait for another day. Or make a quick bread or some muffins. Or read about sourdough.

If you don't have any of the utensils mentioned—improvise!

First You Take Some Yeast . . .

The most critical judgment you make comes at the very beginning, testing the temperature of the water in which you dissolve your yeast. It should be warm, not tepid and not hot—around 100°F. (which is not as hot as it sounds). If you err on the side of coolness, don't worry; it may take a frustratingly long time for the yeast to activate itself, but it will. If you err on the side of hotness, all is lost; the yeast plants die (that's what happens when you put them in the oven) and the dough never rises. If you have a thermometer, you'll save yourself anxiety. If not run the water over your wrist (hands are unreliable); if it feels definitely but not uncomfortably warm, it's okay.

Put two cups warm water in the large mixing bowl. Add the honey and the dry yeast. Stir together. Now leave this alone for a few minutes; it will take about three to fifteen minutes, depending on the temperature of the water. If you're really involved you can sit there and watch it. The grains of yeast will coalesce, then heave up over the surface and eventually foam and froth. If the last part doesn't happen, the water was probably a little cool, but go ahead with the bread anyway. Sometimes you will see almost an explosion of activity, as the swelling yeast spreads over the surface like a mushroom cloud. Exciting. But it might be death throes if the water was too hot.

And Then You Add . . .

When the yeast is bubbly, add the oil, salt and two cups of the flour. The next step is to beat this viscous mixture extremely well. This stimulates early development of gluten, that magic ingredient in the flour which gives your bread lightness and a fine texture. Beating is somewhat boring but just accept it; it will save time in the kneading and is a good investment.

If you have an electric mixer or hand beater, beat the dough on medium speed for about two minutes or longer. Or beat it with a wooden spoon, at least 200 strokes. You can look out the window, listen to the radio, read a book or talk to someone. If your arm gets tired, leave it a few minutes. When you have finished beating, the surface of the dough may have a glossy look. A good sign.

Add the wheat germ and dry milk and mix them in. Then add two to three cups more flour, a little at a time, mixing with a wooden spoon (or dough hook on an electric mixer) until the dough is too stiff to stir and pulls away from the sides of the bowl.

Now You Are Ready to Knead . . .

Kneading is like dancing. Most any way you do it will be okay. Heavy duty mixers with dough hooks knead differently than human hands, but both do a good job. At various times in the past, kneading has been done with feet. For most yeast breads you really don't have to worry about "hurting" the dough. A delicate touch is fine but it will take longer to produce a state of elasticity. Energy and decisiveness will get you there more quickly.

What you are doing is rubbing the cell walls of the **gluten** together so that they will stretch and form an elastic, honeycombed network to hold the carbon dioxide gas produced by the fermenting yeast. As the gas fills the cellular structure it becomes like a sponge filling and expanding with water. This is what is happening as the dough rises.

Choose a kneading surface (bread board, table top or other clean surface) that is about the level of your wrists when your arms are hanging at your sides. Anything higher will tire your shoulders. A counter top is probably too high, unless you are tall.

Sprinkle the surface with flour. Dip your hands in the flour. Dump the dough out of the bowl onto the board. Turn it around and over to coat the outside with flour, patting it to get it to hold together in a cohesive mass. Begin to knead.

Take the far side of the dough and fold it over about ¾ of the way toward you, as though you were folding a sheet of paper, Now, with the heels of your hands (dipped in flour) push the folded portion down and away from you. Give the whole piece of dough a quarter-turn, fold and push. Repeat. Each time you will be folding and pushing a different segment of the dough. Do it over and over. Pretty soon the folding, pushing

THE BASIC LOAF

and turning come together in a rhythmic sequence. Don't worry if it seems jerky in the beginning.

The dough will be rough and sticky at first. You may have to keep dipping your hands in flour. You may have to sprinkle more flour on the dough and on the board. Resign yourself to a little flour wafting through the air and settling on your kitchen floor. Use a pastry scraper to pry the dough up off the board if it really sticks.

Flours vary greatly in moisture content, therefore it is impossible to give the exact amount you will need. Your basic guideline is to add only as much flour as you need to keep the dough from being too sticky to work with. Remember that as the gluten develops the dough will become less sticky and more cohesive. A common mistake for the beginning baker is to overdo the flour, making a dry loaf inevitable. In most cases it is desirable to end up with a dough that is smooth but still soft and pliable.

It's Nearly Ready

After a while the dough will begin to feel resilient. The first few times you may think this will never happen. Have faith. And how do you recognize it when it happens? This is subjective but you will learn with experience. As the dough becomes resilient, it begins to resist your approaches a little; when you push it, it springs back into place. This is what is meant by elasticity. Eventually it will become smooth and satiny on the surface—if it is a white flour dough. Whole wheat and rye flours are inherently more sticky and will continue to cling to your fingers and to the board a little even when they have become elastic. A sure sign that a white flour dough has been kneaded enough is the appearance of blisters just under the skin. Sometimes you can hear the tiny squeal of bubbles popping. Whole wheat doughs will take much longer to reach the blistering stage and you will probably give up before then, but if the dough is quite resilient, it's ready.

Many guidebooks will tell you to knead about 10 minutes. That's a good ball-park figure. I have given no indications of time in this book because it is so dependent on the type of flour you are using, the way and the tempo at which you knead, and whether you are interrupted during the kneading. Don't feel that beginning to knead a dough is a commitment that pre-empts all others. If you get tired or bored or something calls you away, just cover the dough with a towel and come back when you can. You'll probably find it even more cooperative when you return.

Let the Dough Rise . . .

When the dough, as best you can tell, is smooth and elastic, put it into a bowl which is at least twice as big as the piece of dough. First rub the bowl with soft butter or margarine or brush it with melted butter. Oil is less satisfactory as it tends to be absorbed by the dough and the dough then tends to stick to the bowl. Turn the dough over a couple of times so that all sides will be coated with a thin layer of fat, or brush the top of the dough with melted butter. This is to keep it from drying out and a crust forming as it rises. Cover the bowl with a kitchen towel. With whole wheat and rye dough the towel should be dampened because of their stronger tendency to form a crust.

It's customary to place the dough in a warm place. Actually, it doesn't matter much where you put it, as long as the place isn't really hot or subject to drafts. Yeast recoils from drafts like a plant (it is a plant) and this leads to uneven rising. If you put the dough in a cool place it will rise slowly, but it will rise. It will even rise, phlegmatically, in the refrigerator. In a warm place it will rise more rapidly. As you gain experience you will choose your place according to how much time you have.

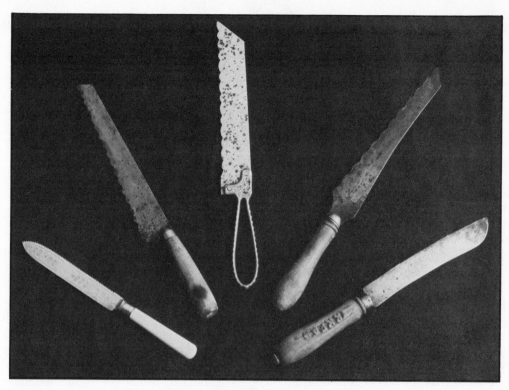

Old bread knives.

Some people feel that the finest grain is developed by a slow, relaxed, lukewarm rising. Others feel that once the yeast is activated the whole procedure should be carried through with optimally warm temperatures and all deliberate speed. Many people recommend the inside of the oven, which may be barely warmed by a pilot light in the case of a gas oven, and is draft-free. If your oven has no pilot light, preheat it for half a minute, turn it off and put the bowl inside. Or put the bowl in the oven with a pan of hot water on the shelf below. Or set the bowl in a cozy corner in a larger bowl of quite warm water.

The warmest place in my cool New England kitchen is on top of the stove, where there is usually some residual heat from the oven having been on. You have to be careful, though. The ideal temperature, on the warm end of the scale, is about 85°F. In many parts of the country that would be a normal kitchen temperature in the summer and putting it on the stove would be too much. If I'm not in a hurry, I'll set the bowl anywhere there's room (out of drafts). Yeast will work all the way down to about 40°-45°, at which point it enters a state of suspended animation.

Rising time will vary, since this depends on the temperature of all the ingredients in the dough, the amount of yeast and the kinds of flour and additives used, the temperature of the bowl, altitude, and the place you set the bowl. It can take anywhere from forty-five minutes to a number of hours.

The next subjective evaluation you have to make is whether the dough has risen to double its bulk. A conventional test is to poke a finger into the top of the dough, about an inch down, and withdraw it. If the hole you have made remains, it has risen enough. As Laura, who wrote the recipe we are following, says, "Let it rise till a punch stays punched." Use it in conjunction with eye judgment. This is much easier in a bowl with fairly straight sides, because if the dough initially filled the bowl halfway, it will have risen enough when it fills the bowl all the way. Don't get nervous; if you don't hit it right on the button, it's not going to make any crucial difference.

Some people like to let the dough overrise somewhat for the lighter texture resulting. If the dough gets away from you and rises to much greater than double, it's best to punch it down and let it rise again in the bowl before you proceed. The finer texture produced by multiple risings compensates for the coarse webbing produced by the initial overrise. You can do this several times, some recipes even call for it, but just remember that it will rise quite a bit faster the second and third times around. And you can't continue indefinitely because the yeast will eventually exhaust itself.

THE BASIC LOAF

Shaping the Loaves . . .

When the dough looks like it has doubled in size and your finger punch remains, give the dough a good sock with your fist. This is called punching the dough down. It will heave a sigh as it collapses. Take it over to your lightly floured board or work surface and dump or pull it out of the bowl. The surface will probably be somewhat greasy, so roll it around on the board. Knead a few times to press out gas bubbles. Don't add any more flour unless for some reason it seems disturbingly sticky. Usually the slight tackiness that lingered when you kneaded the first time will have disappeared and the dough is now lovingly compliant.

After a few kneads, take a sharp knife and cut the dough into two equal pieces. Cover them with your towel and do something else for five to fifteen minutes while the dough "rests." This short "nap" will make the dough easier to form into loaves.

Grease two eight-inch or nine-inch loaf pans. Use soft or melted butter, preferably sweet butter. If you don't have loaf pans, or as a matter of preference, grease a baking sheet and sprinkle it with cornmeal.

People shape loaves differently. Some flatten the dough with a rolling pin and then roll it up jelly-roll fashion. Some just pat it into shape. Experimentation will show the best way for you. This works for me: Take one piece of dough, pat it with your hands into a rough ball and then flatten it to a size about twice as wide as your loaf pan and slightly longer. Don't get out a ruler for this; the size isn't crucial. Now there is probably a smooth area in the middle of your flattened dough—this is what you want to be on top of your loaf. (Loaves with creases running through them taste just as good but fail the pretty test.) Fold the two long sides under so that they meet in the middle of the bottom. Tuck the two short ends under. You now have a loaf. Press it down gently against the board to help the folded dough stick to itself. With your hands, smooth, pat, plump or push slightly, if necessary, just as you would to get a piece of clay into a desired shape. If your loaf looks funny or still has creases running through it, press it out with your hands into a flattened rectangle and try again.

Shaping a free-form oval for a baking sheet is even easier. Just follow the same procedure. End up with a loaf that is oblong, or round and fat, or long and skinny with tapered ends. The shape doesn't matter as long as it's approximately symmetrical.

Carefully place your shaped dough in the loaf pans or on the baking sheet. If necessary, gently press or pat it a little more to get it to reach the ends and sides of the pans. Don't squash it or mangle it with finger marks as the evidence will remain.

If, when the dough is in the pan, you see that it fills the pan more than ½ to ⅔ full, it's probably safest (though you won't want to do it) to take it out and prepare larger pans, or bake the loaves on a baking sheet. Remember that the dough will rise to almost double before it goes in the oven, and then a little more. Loaves that expand somewhat above the pan, mounding up on top and spreading slightly over the sides in the classic loaf profile, are very attractive. But too much dough for the pan can produce bizarre shapes, overflow, and even collapse. Generally speaking it's best not to choose and grease your pans until you have shaped the dough and can tell how large the loaves are.

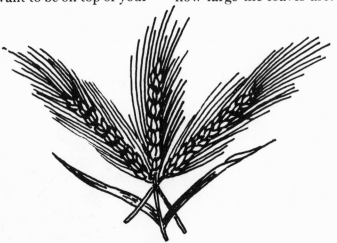

Brush the tops of the loaves with soft or melted butter. (Keeping a small pan of melted butter, with a pastry brush, ready on top of the stove is so useful for so many things in cooking that I no longer consider it troublesome.)

Cover the pans or baking sheet with the towel and put them in a draft-free place to rise.

Preheat the oven to 375°F. in this case. (If you forget and the loaves are suddenly ready to go in, just put them in anyway and turn the oven to 375°F.) Ideally, the loaves should be almost double in size, allowing for the end of the rising in the oven. Don't fret; your guess will be good enough. The dough should look evenly swollen and the pans will feel light when you pick them up. If the dough has definitely doubled that's still okay, but if it's about to fall over the edges of the pans, best to punch it down and reshape the loaves.

These loaves will take about twenty-five to thirty minutes to bake. Resist the impulse to open the oven door and peek during the first fifteen to twenty minutes, even though curiosity will be strong. An opened door may allow 25 percent of the heat to escape.

It is impossible to give exact baking times for bread, just as it is impossible to give exact amounts of flour. It depends on the kinds of pans you use, the amount of flour in your dough, the accuracy of your oven, etc. Here again you depend on judgment. About five minutes before the minimum baking time suggested in the recipe, take a look. If the loaves are in pans, notice if the tops are well browned and the sides have shrunk slightly from the sides of the pan. Remove from the oven. Tap bottom of pan to release loaf. Turn the loaf out into your other, oven-gloved hand. Give the bottom a tap with one fingernail. If it produces a hollow sound, it is done. Try this a few times and you will learn to distinguish the dull thud of an undone loaf from the hollow thump of a done one. With free form loaves, use the same test, lifting the loaf off the baking sheet with a large spatula or pancake turner.

Cool the Bread—If You Can Wait . . .

When done, turn the loaves out on a wire rack in a draft-free place to cool. If you neglect to cool them on a rack, escaping steam will form condensation on the bottom of the loaf and make it soggy.

Sometimes a recipe will call for you to brush the bread with a **glaze** of some sort, either before you put it in the oven or about five to ten minutes before it is done. You don't have to wait for the suggestion; glaze a loaf whenever you feel like it. On the other hand, if a recipe calls for it and you don't feel like it, forget it.

When you take the loaves out, if they seem to have very dark and/or hard crusts (this often happens with whole wheat recipes), you may want to brush them with melted butter to soften the crust. The same result can be obtained by covering the loaves with a towel as they cool on the rack. The towel will not prevent steam from escaping. If you want a crusty crust, don't do either of these things.

In any case, don't wrap the bread in such a way that steam can't escape until it is thoroughly cool. This takes several hours. If you must take the bread somewhere, put it in a paper bag, a plastic bag left open, or wrap it loosely in a kitchen towel.

Bread doesn't slice well when it's hot, but the suspense may be too strong to wait. Don't be disappointed if it's a bit doughy inside. The texture will improve in an hour or two and it may even still be warm.

This recipe makes two loaves. Happy eating.

A CHECK LIST

Sometimes when you're doing things that involve many steps which aren't too familiar, it's helpful to make an abbreviated list to put within eye's reach. This saves struggling through the complete directions again in search of one point of information. Here is a list for yeast bread:

bowl
yeast/water
wait
add everything but flour
mix
add some flour
beat
add flour
turn out
knead
rise in bowl
double
punch down
turn out
knead briefly
cut and cover
rest
grease pans
shape dough
butter tops
rise again
preheat
bake
test done
cool on rack
eat

THE HARRIED BAKER

Often one hears the plaintive words: I would love to make my own bread, but I just don't have the time, not with my job . . . house . . . children . . . social commitments. . . . Untrue. Anyone who does more than just pass through his or her home once a day has the time to make bread.

Overnight in the Fridge

Let's say you are a person with a full-time job. If you can find 30 minutes at night, that's all it takes to get a yeast dough mixed, kneaded and into its large buttered bowl. The dough can rise overnight in the refrigerator. You don't even need special recipes for this. Use a little more yeast, say one and one-half tablespoons instead of the one tablespoon listed in the recipe. Brush the top of the dough liberally with melted butter and cover with a damp towel. (Refrigerators dry things out.) If you have time, let the dough stand on the countertop fifteen to thirty minutes to give the yeast a good start before putting it in the refrigerator; if not, put it in right away.

After Work and Ready for the Oven

If you're the sort who gets up early, take the dough out before breakfast, punch it down and let it rest while you have breakfast. Form into loaves, put them in greased pans, butter tops, return to refrigerator and cover with damp towel. When you get home that night take the loaves out. If they haven't risen quite enough, let them finish in a warm place. If they have risen enough, let them sit at room temperature for ten minutes while you pre-heat the oven. If you're in a rush, put them directly into the cold oven and turn it on to the temperature called for.

If you don't have time to make the dough into loaves in the morning, punch it down, cover with damp towel, and return to the refrigerator. I do not recommend covering the bowl with plastic wrap. Should the dough rise to the plastic and meet resistance it may fall back on itself and turn sour.

Bee Hive

Bread Before Bed

You can also condense the bread-making process. If you are home by 6:30 p.m. you can bake a bread by 10:30 p.m. with time during risings for other things. Choose a recipe calling for white flour. Have all ingredients and utensils at room temperature. Mix the yeast in water that is between 100° and 110°F. Arrange a warm cozy place for the dough to rise.

Or. . . Take the dough through its first rising, form into loaves, place in pans, butter tops, cover with damp towel and refrigerate overnight. Allow time to bake them before you leave in the morning. If you can't, check to see how much they have risen. If loaves look quite puffy, punch them down, re-shape, return to pans, cover and refrigerate. Bake them that evening.

Home But Not Free

If you are a person with children and are home most of the time, your schedule is probably more erratic but also more flexible. With small children, you may think finding even the thirty minutes to start the bread is wishful thinking. But bread-making is not an unforgiving procedure like making a soufflé. You've undoubtedly learned to put things down and come back to them as the myriad urgencies of children interrupt your every impulse. Fine, the bread won't mind. At virtually any point you can abandon the dough as is or perhaps slip it into the refrigerator. If you've just begun, you can leave the yeast in its warm water for long enough to deal with any but major emergencies. If you've begun adding the other ingredients you have a "sponge," which many people like to let sit around for a while anyway. If you must leave here, try to add about 2 cups of flour. This you can stir in in a few seconds. Make a habit of using a large mixing bowl so, if left, the sponge won't bubble up over the top.

If you're called away in the midst of kneading, throw a towel over the dough. You'll find it even more malleable when you come back. If the dough rose too much, punch it down, knead it again briefly, re-grease your bowl if necessary and let it rise again. You can do this several times if you have to. Each time it will rise a little faster.

If you've finished kneading and have to leave for an extended period, put the bowl in the refrigerator. Follow the precautions mentioned earlier, brushing the top liberally with melted butter and covering with a damp towel to keep a crust from forming on the top. If you don't get back until the next day, that's all right too.

If something happens while the bread is in the oven, you do have a problem. If it's far enough along, turn off the oven and hope it will finish baking in the residual heat. If it is almost done, take it out.

Another option you have is to freeze the dough, either as an unrisen lump, wrapped in plastic, or formed into loaves. Place the loaves in their well-greased pans into the freezer and, when frozen, slide the loaves out of the pans and wrap in plastic. Put them back into pans when you take them out to thaw and rise (which takes about half a day). Frozen dough doesn't remain viable much longer than two weeks.

Obviously I have not thought of all the things which can happen to interrupt you or all the ways you can handle them. As you work bread-making into the fabric of your life, you will find your own ways to adapt and improvise. The versatility and anticipation involved are worth it for the satisfactions you will both find and give with your own, real bread.

Different stone-ground grains from five different mills
(of the Vermont Country Store Grist Mill Museum).

BEYOND, BEFORE AND BESIDES YEAST BREAD: A PLETHORA OF CATEGORIES

Batter Breads, or How to Have Yeast Bread without Exerting Yourself

Face it, some people just don't enjoy kneading, even enough to make homemade bread. But there is another way, batter breads which are beaten, not kneaded. How much depends on your stamina and patience. The minimal effort will still produce a tasty bread. If you're lucky enough to have a heavy-duty mixer you can get superb breads with practically no effort at all on your part.

Batter breads are different and ingratiating, with a thick crunchy crust, coarse crumb, chewy texture and cratered surface like a lava flow. Their homely apearance (for they lack the symmetry of kneaded breads) and yeasty flavor (they need more yeast because the gluten that supports rising is not completely developed by kneading) make them more elemental than elegant.

The Longer the Beating the Better

The method for batter breads is to add some of the flour to the yeast and liquids, and beat as with regular breads, only longer. With a heavy-duty mixer you can add enough flour to make a thick, viscous batter. If you're using a hand mixer, add only as much as can be beaten without straining the motor. If you're beating by hand, you'll have to be the judge of how thick a batter is beatable. With an electric mixer beat the dough five minutes, or longer. By hand, beat as long as you can and then ask someone else to take over. (You get the idea.)

Gradually add enough more flour to form a dough that clings together, yet can still be pushed around with a wooden spoon. You can do all of this and even continue beating for a few more minutes with a heavy-duty mixer. You will think the batter is very stiff and hard to handle but it is actually a much looser dough than the kneaded one. It remains as pully as taffy but should have some degree of elasticity.

Two Risings Improve Texture

Let the dough rise in the bowl you mixed it in until it has doubled in bulk. It isn't necessary to grease the bowl or the top of the dough. Stir it down with a spoon. (This is the same as punching down a kneaded dough.) Spoon into buttered pans. This is sometimes the hardest part. You'll have to push and pull, using the spoon and probably your fingers. Whatever configurations or crevasses are in the dough will remain right through the baking, so try to urge it into the corners of the pan and get it reasonably smooth on top. Allow to rise in a warm place. As with other yeast doughs, any part of the rising can be slowed by putting it in the refrigerator. Cover with a damp towel. The texture of batter breads is improved by two risings but one rising (in the pans) will suffice, especially if the craving for fresh bread strikes an hour and a half before dinner.

Select a baking pan which the dough fills halfway. If you get the dough in and it's much under or over that, take it out and find another pan. Let the dough rise until it reaches the top of the pan, then pop it in the oven.

Return to Oven for Crisper Crust

I like to bake these breads in their pans until they pass the tap test for doneness, then take them out and put them directly on the oven rack for three to five minutes. This produces a crisp crust all over, and these breads are noteworthy for their crusts.

A nice quality of batter breads is that they can be eaten while hot. Just let them sit on a rack for about ten minutes before slicing. Lucky is the person who gets the end slice. Batter breads are best the day they are baked, but most make superior toast if they last. Some are even better toasted than fresh.

In theory, almost any regular yeast bread could become a batter bread. Double the yeast, beat very thoroughly, stop adding flour when the dough is too stiff to beat and pulls together, and skip the kneading. Conversely, by reducing the yeast and continuing through the kneading process, batter breads can become conventional yeast breads. So disavow categorical thinking and experiment in one of the most versatile areas of bread-making.

A postscript: For small households or those who feel beating three cups of flour is easier than six (it is, somewhat), the batter bread recipes in this book have been planned so that they could be conveniently halved to make one loaf instead of two.

Quick Breads

Quick breads are almost effortless, straightforward and versatile. Anything can go into them. Invent your own, but before you do, master a couple of tested recipes so that the procedure becomes second nature to you.

Most quick breads:

>are sweeter than most yeast breads.
>contain fruits and/or nuts.
>are leavened with baking powder and/or baking soda.
>have a crumbly, often crunchy texture.
>are usually served with tea or coffee as a snack or dessert; some go well with meals.
>make good toast and a few can be used for sandwiches.

All the quick-bread recipes follow the same procedure, which is the simplest one I know.
Rules are few and steps are short.

Rules:

Sift dry ingredients so that the leaveners and spices will be evenly distributed.

Add dry ingredients to wet ingredients all at once. Stir with a few quick strokes to blend. Batter will be slightly lumpy. Don't be concerned; too vigorous mixing will result in a tough loaf.

Batters should be mushy, not runny and not stiff. You can make adjustments: If batter seems too thin, sprinkle in a few tablespoons of flour. If batter seems too stiff, so that it's hard to get the dry ingredients mixed in, add a little more of the liquid called for.

Note:

Flour measurements are given exactly, but remember, flours vary in the amount of moisture they contain and will absorb. A stiff batter makes a dry, terrible bread.

Use greased pans.

Fill pans about two-thirds full.

Bake between 325° and 350°F. Most breads bake in forty-five minutes to an hour.

To check for doneness:

(1) Look at the bread. See if the top is beginning to look brown, and the sides are pulling away slightly from the sides of the pan.

(2) Stick a toothpick or cake tester in the middle of the loaf. It should come out clean.

I now depend mainly on the touch test, along with the appearance of the loaf. So that you will know what it should not feel like, about halfway through the baking time, reach into the oven and push down gently on the top of the loaf with your finger. It will be squishy. When the loaf is done it will feel springy. The top will give slightly and you can sense there is softness remaining underneath, but not mush. It is resilient but tender. If there is resistence or firmness to your push, it is probably overdone. Keep in mind that you are making a very different kind of judgment than you would with a yeast bread where the crust is crisp and hard. Quick breads are supposed to be moist with a tender crust. They will be soft when taken from the oven. Yeast breads soften somewhat as they cool. Quick breads firm up.

Let the bread cool in its pan ten to fifteen minutes so it will slip out more easily and without falling apart. Don't try to slice it right away but you don't have to wait as long as with yeast breads. It will be crumbly, but that shouldn't stand between you and enjoyment.

Steps:
1. Preheat oven.
2. Mix together the liquid ingredients in a large bowl.
3. Add fruits and/or nuts, if called for.
4. Sift together all dry ingredients.
5. Add dry ingredients to wet ingredients. Mix together gently with a wooden spoon or rubber spatula until just blended.
6. Pour into greased pan.
7. Bake until various tests suggest doneness.
8. Leave bread in pan for ten to fifteen minutes.
9. Turn out on rack to cool.

Corn Breads

First, it was a mainstay in the diet of native American Indians—then, for over a hundred years, corn was the basic grain in colonial baking. Now, while cornmeal still has its passionate regional adherents, it is more peripheral than central to everyday American cooking. Yet, along with sourdough, corn bread is the most American of all breads. Since the grain is versatile, flavorful and moderately nutritious, I would like to rekindle an interest in its use.

Cornmeal Unlimited

The concept of corn bread is nothing if not flexible. Take a little meal, a little water and maybe some salt and you can make johnnycakes (fried on a griddle), hoe cakes (baked on a hoe over an open fire), ash cakes (baked in the ashes), or corn pones (in an oven or on a griddle). Fancy the batter up with milk, fat, eggs, sweetening, seasonings, herbs, spices, fruits, nuts, leavening or other flours and you have latter-day griddle cakes, gems, muffins, waffles, spoon bread, or corn bread. All are variations on a theme. What you end up with depends on the proportion of liquid to dry and the manner in which you cook it. You can substitute or add in most of these recipes, vary the equation of flour and meal, and use either white or yellow cornmeal.

One can heartily recommend stone-ground, whole-grain cornmeal, it is available in health food and specialty stores, at many small mills and from mail order catalogues. Stone-ground meal makes a bread which is grainier than that from the bland, degerminated meal sold in the supermarket. It isn't as tender but has greater character and superior nutritional qualities.

Leftover corn bread should never be thrown away. It makes sumptuous toast, split, buttered and browned under the broiler. Serve with jam for breakfast or tea.

Corn bread makes superb stuffing for turkeys or other large birds (the best, according to Southerners). Freeze it until you need it, then thaw, crumble and mix with whatever else you use to make stuffing. It's well worth making corn bread, a day in advance, just to have it for stuffing.

An old Southern custom is to break leftover corn bread into chunks, pour milk over it, and eat it like cereal. My mother often did this for supper. I saw it with my own eyes. I'm not necessarily recommending, just documenting.

Steamed Breads

Say steamed bread and everybody thinks of Boston brown bread, something you eat with baked beans. Actually, you can use many combinations of ingredients. It's a method, not a recipe, and a useful one to have in your repertoire since it allows you to make bread on top of the stove, on a hot plate, in a fireplace or on an open fire. The traditional way is to cook the breads in cans, often coffee cans, in a large pot of simmering water. An alternative is to put the batter in the top of a double boiler (fill about halfway), and cook over boiling water for the same period of time. And if you don't have cans or a double boiler, you can always tie it in cloth and suspend it over boiling water.

Be Inventive

Steamed breads often call for a combination of flours or grains and usually include cornmeal. Fruits and nuts go well in them. Their texture is at once velvety/grainy, with the grainy dominating as they cool. If you're off in a cabin on an island and the only ingredients you have are not in the following recipes, don't be thwarted. Experimentation is productive. Not every combination will turn out to be appealing (on the other hand, something which sounds a little strange may be delightful). Occasionally you will find a formula which, if only the world knew, is a true addition to bread lore.

A few things to keep in mind:

You can steam bread in any old can that happens to be around, not just the one-lb. coffee cans often specified. You'll have to adjust the cooking time for smaller or larger sizes.

The batter should fill the can about two-thirds full, certainly not more than three-fourths as it will either overflow or be squelched. If it is much less than two-thirds full the top may stay mushy from condensation.

One teaspoon of leavening (baking powder or soda) is a reasonable amount for a one-pound coffee-can loaf. As for proportion of liquid to solid, the batter should have a consistency somewhere between oozing and pouring. I would rather err a little on the wet side since you can always cook it longer, but a bread that's too dry is pretty much a waste. The ingredients in a batter determine how loose the batter will be (cornmeal, for instance, absorbs a lot of moisture). Doing it is the only way to find out.

The recipes included can be easily halved to make one coffee-can loaf instead of two. You might want to make two or three different ones at the same time. A large canning kettle will hold three coffee cans without their touching each other.

Some people like to use the plastic tops that come with coffee cans instead of tying on foil. Plastic tops are easy and tight, but there is the possibility that a batter may rise enough to force off the top; therefore, I usually prefer foil (which will stay on even if it is forced up a bit). The foil "caps" can be saved and re-used until they get punctured.

Put the cans in the boiling water bath with a rack under them. Check several times to make sure the simmering point has been established. Letting them boil instead of simmer will produce tough results. Once the heat is right, you can pretty much forget them. Just take a note of what time you put them in so they won't simmer on interminably.

Don't be put off by the hours of cooking. Most of that time you aren't even involved.

It is lovely to plan a batch of steamed bread so that you can serve it hot for a meal. It is extremely moist and tender right out of the pot. The old-fashioned way of slicing the bread when hot is to tie a string around the loaf and pull the ends together to cut through.

If not eating at once, cool and slice the bread thinly in rounds. Serve with sweet butter, whipped cream cheese or cottage cheese. The last, with its fresh tartness, is a pleasing complement to the dark mellow sweetness of many steamed breads.

Steamed breads keep well, wrapped in plastic. You can also slice the loaf thinly and freeze it. To use, thaw, wrap it in foil and warm in a low oven. Steamed breads make quite pleasant toast.

Antique dough bowl.

Old dough mixing bucket.

Little Breads

Little breads are just that: anything which can be devoured in a few bites. They encompass such delectables as biscuits, rolls and muffins. Any dough which can be made into yeast bread will do for rolls. Shape it into tiny rounds instead of loaves and bake for a shorter time. Some recipes are favorites for miniatures and we have included several.

Fried Breads

Some of our more sumptuous earthly delights are among the humble fried breads. Mostly small, they are both deep fried and griddle-fried. The range is so wide they seem hardly related, running a gamut from scones to pancakes to fritters to English muffins to Indian chappattis—and more. Self-discipline has been known to wither at the first innocent bite of a warm doughnut. Caveat dieter.

Sweet and Festive Breads

Breads for holidays or special times of your own invention are a folk art in themselves. Often associated with a particular culture and season, they are highly evolved in their specialization. Frugality is banished here. Usually rich and somewhat sweet, they employ an abundance of ingredients and embellishments. In shapes whimsical, symbolic or bizarre, elaborations are unlimited. In mastering these breads, patience and a deft touch are helpful as they are not easy, but there is no more personal way to honor a celebration with hands and heart.

Sourdough Breads

Yeast-leavened breads as we know them are an invention of the more recent past. For thousands of years before, bread was leavened by tearing off a piece of dough and using it to **start** the next day's batch.

Sometimes starters were made with a yeast derived from hops, the ancestor of our present commercial yeast, and sometimes with a wild strain captured from the air. Wild yeast became identified with and almost mythologized by American pioneers who eventually adopted the generic name, "sourdough."

These peripatetic frontiersmen carried a starter with them, usually in a wooden pail which became permeated with the culture and would retain the life of the yeast even if the starter spilled. A more solid mass might be cushioned, womb-like, in a bag of flour or under one's jacket to keep it warm. Starters were jealously guarded as freshly baked bread, biscuits or pancakes often provided the only variety in the wilderness diet. In addition there was the alcoholic by-product called "hooch," the clear liquid which rises to the top of the starter and had its own uses.

Antique bread mixer.

That Indescribable Something

My first sourdough starter, I was told and chose to believe, was an old and precious culture which first crossed the continent in a covered wagon. A hundred years later, a jar of it was hand-carried back East on a jet plane, with stops along the way where it survived freezing nights on hotel window sills. It was a sweet and bubbly strain, belying its vintage. Some years later it met an untimely demise. At present there are three jars of starter in my refrigerator, each one different in aroma and flavor, but none equals the original's vigor and charm.

The dramatic, earthy character of sourdoughs makes them possibly the most exciting breads of all. They speak of beginnings, of roots and of things unknowable. For these reasons did nineteenth century housewives call their starters "witches' yeast."

Wild vs. Tame

Sourdough is a very different plant from commercial yeast. Breads made with it are coarser and chewier with a heavier crust. The taste is distinctively tangy or "sour." There are wide variations in sourdough breads, depending on the particular characteristics of the starter, the incubation period of the "sponge," and other ingredients used. For some people sourdough is an acquired taste; for many it is almost an addiction. Sourdoughs can be adjusted to be milder and sweeter or stronger and more sour, but you can never quite reduce it to a formula. Each loaf will be individual. Sometimes there will be disappointment; sometimes revelation; and therein lies the fun.

The difference between sourdough and commercial yeast is something like the difference between a housecat and a tiger. Commercial "tame" yeast is standardized and reliable. For sourdough starters yeast spores are enticed from their free-floating state in the atmosphere into a hospitable environment. Once captured, with care, they will replenish themselves forever.

To Create A Starter

The simplest starters rely on flour and water; others use additional ingredients. Sometimes even commercial yeast is added.

> Flours—any kind can be used: white, whole wheat, rye, buckwheat
>
> Liquids—several different ones can be used: water, potato water, whole or skim milk

Crucial Factors include the presence of **Starch** (flours) on which the yeast feeds, **Moisture** (liquids) to attract the yeast (if the medium is too dry it will mold) and **Patience** as it can take two to seven days for fermentation to get going.

You Have Succeeded when the starter smells decidedly sour, is frothy and light and a clear liquid rises to the top. Put it in a large jar and refrigerate.

However, if it does not bubble, or if it molds or just dries up and smells awful, consign it to the compost. I have tried all the recipes which follow and had the best luck with the Honey Starter, but your experience may be completely different. Be forewarned that, even when you succeed, making your own starter is a gamble. The micro-organisms you attract on a particular day may be wild and delicious, or relatively characterless, or quite unpleasant, even though all will bubble and froth and raise your bread. I'm not one who can resist that kind of gamble, but the **surest** way to a good starter with sourdough is to beg some from a friend who has a starter of proven quality.

Recently, dried starters have become available in some health food and specialty stores. These look much like granulated yeast and come with directions for reconstituting. The full flavor of your yeast, however you acquire it, will not reveal itself until it has "seasoned" for a week or two. For this reason it makes sense to keep a jar of starter ready in your refrigerator rather than going through the process of creation each time.

Care and Feeding

Keep the starter in a closed container of glass, plastic or crockery. Never use metal. Unless the container is at least twice as large as the volume of starter, don't screw the top on tightly, especially in the case of glass, or the expanding starter may actually burst the container. Messy, but better to just have it froth out all over your refrigerator. I suggest a container of one to two quarts. This allows you to keep enough starter that you can use frequently without unduly diminishing its vitality and necessitating a long recovery period.

Sourdough Breads

Making A Sponge

People use various methods when working with sourdough. The method I prefer is this: A day or two before baking, make a sponge as directed in each recipe. This will be a portion of your starter plus a fresh amount of flour and liquid. Stir together in a large crockery, glass or plastic bowl. It will be lumpy and thick at first, but will blend and thin as it works. Cover the bowl. Let it sit six hours or overnight. The recipes in this book specify a wait of up to forty-eight hours.

The temperature and the length of time you let the sponge sit will determine the degree of fermentation and thus the sourness of the final product. After several hours you will notice the mixture rising and forming bubbles (carbon dioxide) and it will begin to smell sour and fermented. The longer you allow this process to go on the stronger flavor the sourdough will have. For a milder taste, let the sponge sit for only six to eight hours or:

Add ½ teaspoon baking soda.
Increase the sweetening agent in the recipe.
Add a tablespoon of sugar directly to your starter each time you feed it.

I like to use a commercial yeast to boost the leavening action of the sourdough. I have not found that in the small quantity called for it detracts from the sourdough's distinctiveness.

Next, add all other ingredients except the flour. Amounts of flour called for are even more approximate in sourdough baking because of the amount of liquid produced during fermentation.

Add flour until the dough becomes too stiff to stir. Turn it out and proceed with kneading. Sourdoughs will take longer to rise than other doughs. This can be hastened by the addition of soda or commercial yeast. Sourdoughs can be refrigerated, allowed to rise overnight, and baked the next day.

Warning: Sourdoughs are fragile and any temperature over 95°F. is lethal.

Feeding the Starter Means Just That

As was mentioned earlier, the yeast must have starch to feed on in order to remain active. If you are using your starter frequently and replacing it as the recipes direct, this will be sufficient. If you do not use your starter for a week or as long as a month then you are going to have to feed it occasionally.

To do this blend: 1 cup flour
1 cup warm liquid
(milk or water)
sugar, optional

Remove one-half to one cup of the original starter. Throw it out, give it away, or use it. Stir in the fresh flour-liquid mixture with a wooden spoon or rubber spatula and let mixture sit at room temperature for several hours. Stir and refrigerate. It can be returned to the refrigerator immediately if necessary.

You don't have to be a slave to your starter. My first batch came with directions for feeding it every week. This I did diligently until I found I could keep it up to a month in the refrigerator without feeding. The starter will separate and liquid will rise to the top. Stir well, add a fresh quantity of flour and liquid and let sit at room temperature for some hours. If it expands and foams, all is well. If nothing happens, you've probably lost it. Toss it out and don't procrastinate next time.

You will find sourdough baking one of the most flexible methods available to you. The one thing you can't do is hurry it. If you must have something sourdough right away, make quick breads or biscuits or cornbread.

HOMEMADE SOURDOUGH STARTERS

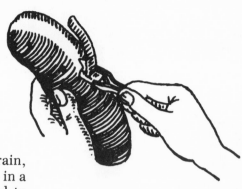

1— Flourless Potato Starter

   3 medium potatoes
   4 cups water
   1 tablespoon dry yeast
   3 tablespoons sugar or honey

   Cook potatoes in the water until soft. Drain, saving the water. Mash the potatoes, or puree in a blender. When the cooking water has cooled to lukewarm, put it in a large glass, plastic or crockery bowl. Add the other ingredients, including the mashed potatoes. Stir to mix. Cover with a towel, and let it sit in a warm place, not over 90°F., for two days or longer. When the mixture is frothy and smells sour, place in a covered container and store in the refrigerator.

2—Potato Water Starter

   1 tablespoon dry yeast
   2 teaspoons sugar
   2 cups warm water in which
      potatoes have been
      cooked
   2 additional cups water
   2 cups unbleached white
      flour, or other flour of
      your choice

   Dissolve the yeast and sugar in the warm potato water. Put in a glass, plastic, or crockery bowl; cover with towel and let it sit in a warm place for about forty-eight hours. At the end of this time stir in 2 more cups warm water and 2 cups flour. Cover. Let it stand overnight or longer, until the whole mixture is frothy and smells sour. Make sure your bowl is large enough to allow for expansion. Store in a covered jar in the refrigerator.

3—Milk Starter Without Yeast

   3 cups milk, whole or
      skimmed
   2 cups unbleached white
      flour

   Let the milk stand in a glass, plastic or crockery bowl, covered, twenty-four hours. Stir in the flour, cover and let stand for several days in a warm place. When the mixture is bubbly and smells sour, store in a covered jar in the refrigerator. For a little extra insurance (not for the purist), add one tablespoon sugar and one-half tablespoon dry yeast with the flour.

HOMEMADE SOURDOUGH STARTERS

4—Raw Potato Starter Without Yeast

1 cup warm water
1 teaspoon honey
1 cup unbleached white
    flour
1 cup raw, peeled, grated
    potato (about one
    medium large potato)

Combine all ingredients in a plastic, glass or crockery bowl. Cover with towel and let sit in a warm place for several days, until foamy and soured. Don't get impatient; it may take three to seven days. Store in a covered jar in the refrigerator.

5—Honey Starter With Yeast

1 tablespoon dry yeast
2 tablespoons honey
2 cups warm water
2 cups unbleached white
    flour

Dissolve the yeast and honey in the water in a glass, plastic or crockery bowl. Stir in the flour. Cover with a towel and let sit in a warm place for several days or until foamy and soured. Store in a covered jar in the refrigerator.

Bee Hive

Note:
With all of these starters, but especially the ones containing yeast, make sure that the bowl is large enough to contain what may be a startling degree of expansion.

January

SPROUTED WHEAT BREAD

In the depths of winter our only access to fresh growing things may be to sprouts. If you keep a garden in a jar, use some of your harvest for this chewy bread which is about as close to the earth, and to spring, as one can get in January.

1½ cups milk

¼ cup oil or melted butter

¼ cup honey

2 tablespoons unsulphured molasses

2 teaspoons salt

1½ tablespoons dry yeast

½ cup warm water

½ teaspoon sugar or honey

3 cups unbleached white flour, approximately

2-2¼ cups wheat sprouts (½ cup wheat berries sprouted)*

3 cups stone ground whole wheat flour

In a saucepan scald the milk; add the oil or butter, honey, molasses and salt. Cool to lukewarm. In a large mixing bowl dissolve the yeast in the warm water with a half-teaspoon honey or sugar.

When yeast solution is bubbly, add the milk mixture and beat. Add 3 cups white flour and beat about 2 minutes with an electric mixer or at least 200 strokes by hand.

Chop the sprouts coarsely. (This isn't really necessary but it helps to get them separated, as they usually cling to each other like a mass of angel's hair.) Mix in.

Add whole wheat flour; mix until the dough pulls away from the sides of the bowl. If this doesn't happen, add a little more white flour.

Turn out onto a board dusted with white flour and knead until smooth and elastic, sprinkling on a little more white flour if the dough remains too sticky. When it starts to become resilient but is still holding on to your fingers, stop adding flour and knead a bit longer. Place dough in a buttered bowl and turn over to coat underside or brush top with melted butter. Cover with a dampened kitchen towel and let it rise until dough has doubled in size.

Punch the dough down, turn it out onto the board and knead a few times. Divide in half, cover with the towel and let rest 10-15 minutes.

Butter two large loaf pans or casseroles. Shape dough to fit, put in pans, brush tops with melted butter, cover with the towel and let rise again until doubled.

Preheat oven to 350°F. Bake about 45 to 50 minutes, or until the bottom of a loaf sounds hollow when tapped.

Cool loaves on a rack.

Makes two loaves.

To sprout wheat berries: Take ½ cup berries (which are available in health food stores) and put in a clean large jar (about 1½ to 2 quarts). Cover the top with cheesecloth secured with a rubber band. Fill the jar with tepid water, put in a dark cozy place (out of drafts) overnight. In the morning, drain and fill again with tepid water and drain immediately. Set the jar somewhere out of direct light. Later in the day repeat the filling with water and draining. You may begin to see tiny sprouts. This is the first day.

On the second day, repeat the filling and draining two or three times when you happen to think of it. The sprouts are definitely growing now, or are they? On the third day repeat the filling and draining again two or three times. The sprouts are getting long now. You can use them, but they'll probably be better if you wait until the fourth day. Try to do one of your washings each night before you go to bed as it's easy for them to dry out overnight.

This whole process may sound complicated, but once you've done it you'll take it completely for granted. The sprouting berries should smell fresh and taste sweet; if they smell sour they have been too warm or too wet. Any leftover sprouts will keep for several days in a container in the refrigerator.

WHOLE WHEAT GRANOLA COFFEECAKE

Rich but not too sweet. A robust treat for Sunday breakfasts.

Preheat oven to 375°F. Sift together the white flour, baking soda and salt. Mix in the whole wheat flour with a fork. In a large bowl beat the egg until very light; add the buttermilk, melted butter and maple syrup and beat well to blend. Add the flour mixture and fold in gently until just combined. Spread batter smoothly in a buttered 8-inch square pan or its equivalent.

Sprinkle with topping.

Topping: Toss first five ingredients with a fork. Drizzle butter over all and toss again.

Bake the coffeecake about 25 minutes or until a toothpick thrust into the cake part comes out clean. Serve warm from the pan with sweet butter. To reheat cover with foil.

Makes one coffeecake.

½ cup unbleached white flour

1 teaspoon baking soda

½ teaspoon salt

1¼ cup whole wheat flour, preferably stone-ground

1 egg

1 cup buttermilk or sour milk

¼ cup melted sweet butter

¼ cup maple syrup (**Honey** may be substituted but will not give as nice a texture. Or use brown sugar and reduce the whole wheat flour to 1 cup.)

Topping:

¼ cup whole wheat flour

¼ cup brown sugar

¾ cup granola (homemade or the best and freshest you can buy)

½ cup chopped pecans or walnuts

1 teaspoon cinnamon

¼ cup melted sweet butter

Selling homemade doughnuts at a roadside stand in Maine.

ORANGE-GLAZED WHOLE WHEAT DOUGHNUTS

Delectable, and healthy enough to justify the loss of control you will probably experience when you see, touch, smell and taste them.

In a large bowl dissolve yeast in the half-cup warm water with the half-teaspoon sugar or honey.

When the yeast is bubbling actively, add the second half-cup water, butter, eggs, honey, salt, cinnamon and cloves. Beat well to mix. Add the 2 cups white flour and beat 2 minutes with an electric mixer or 200 strokes by hand. Gradually add the whole wheat flour until the dough is too stiff to beat and pulls away from the sides of the bowl. Turn the dough out onto a floured board and knead until smooth and elastic, adding a little more whole wheat flour as necessary if it remains persistently sticky. Be patient; give the gluten time to develop; add as little flour as possible. A dough on the soft side is preferred; if you let it get too stiff you'll have dry doughnuts. When the dough reaches a stage of good elasticity but is still slightly tacky, be satisfied.

Put the dough into a buttered bowl, turn it over to coat all sides. Cover with a dampened kitchen towel and let it rise until double in bulk. Punch the dough down, turn out onto a lightly floured board; knead a few times to press out air bubbles. Cover the dough and let it rest for about 10 minutes.

With a floured rolling pin roll out the dough to a thickness of about ½ inch. This may be easier if you do only half the dough at a time. Cut out doughnuts with a medium to large doughnut cutter or two biscuit cutters (one large, one small), dipping the cutters in flour each time. Place the doughnuts and holes on baking sheets or some other surface very lightly dusted with flour. Gather up the scraps of dough, form into a ball and roll out again to cut more doughnuts.

Let the doughnuts and holes rise, uncovered, until almost double in size.

Meanwhile heat several inches of cooking oil in a deep pot to 375° F. Use a candy thermometer if you have one and leave it in the pot so you can constantly monitor the temperature.

Carefully, so as not to deflate them, lift the doughnuts onto a spatula and slide them, one at a time, into the hot oil. Cook only a few at a time; don't crowd the pot! Fry until deep golden brown on both sides, about 3 minutes. It's easier to overdo than underdo, so watch it. They should be slightly moist inside. Remove with a slotted spoon and drain on paper towels (or, following an old tradition, on brown paper bags). Break open one of the first ones to check for proper doneness. Continue frying the remaining doughnuts and holes.

Mix the glaze ingredients. When the doughnuts have cooled slightly, dribble or brush the glaze over them, covering the sides as well as the top. The sweetness of the doughnuts comes mainly from the glaze, which also provides a piquant contrast to the wheatiness of the dough, so you want each one to have a liberal brushing.

These are best while warm, still fine when cool, will not be shunned the next day, and freeze well.

Makes about 20 doughnuts.

½ cup warm water
1½ tablespoons dry yeast
½ teaspoon sugar or honey
½ cup water
¼ cup melted sweet butter (½ stick)
3 eggs
3 tablespoons honey
1 teaspoon salt
¼ teaspoon cinnamon
⅛ teaspoon ground cloves
2 cups unbleached white flour
3 cups, approximately, whole wheat flour, preferably stone-ground
Cooking oil

For glaze:
1 cup confectioners' sugar
1 teaspoon grated orange peel
4 tablespoons orange juice

SOUR CREAM BANANA BREAD

As everyone knows, this is what you do with bananas that are past their prime. Sometimes it's worth letting them get that way on purpose. This bread is light, moist and evil with calories.

1 egg

⅔ cup sour cream

⅓ cup honey, ½ cup sugar

1 teaspoon vanilla

1½ cups very ripe bananas, mashed

1 cup chopped walnuts or pecans

2¼ cups unbleached white flour

1½ teaspoons baking powder

1 teaspoon baking soda

½ teaspoon salt

½ teaspoon cinnamon

Preheat the oven to 350°F.

In a mixing bowl beat the eggs until light. Add the sour cream, honey and vanilla and beat again. Add the bananas and mix well. Stir in the nuts.

Sift together the flour, baking power, baking soda, cinnamon and salt.

Combine with egg mixture and stir gently until just mixed. Pour into a large greased loaf pan.

Bake one to one and one-quarter hours. Banana bread doesn't really test done with a toothpick. Push down gently on the top with your finger; when it's no longer squishy and feels springy, it's probably done. If there's firm resistance, it's probably overdone.

Leave in the pan for about 10 minutes before removing to cool on a wire rack.

Makes one large loaf.

CORN MEAL PECAN WAFFLES

1 cup unbleached white flour

1 teaspoon salt

2 teaspoons baking powder

1 cup cornmeal, preferably stone-ground

3 eggs, separated and at room temperature

1 cup milk

6 tablespoons melted sweet butter

¼ cup maple syrup (or honey)

1 cup chopped pecans or other nuts

Preheat waffle iron.

Sift together the flour, salt and baking powder. Add the cornmeal and mix well with a fork.

In a clean, dry bowl beat the egg whites until they form fairly stiff peaks (don't let them get dry).

In another bowl, with the same beater, beat the egg yolks. Add the milk, butter and maple syrup and beat to mix well. Stir in the chopped pecans. Add the flour mixture and combine it thoroughly. Fold in the beaten egg whites with a rubber spatula.

Pour enough batter on the hot waffle iron to almost cover it when it spreads out, and cook until golden and crisp.

As the remaining batter sits it will thicken somewhat, so you may want to add a little more milk. This amount makes 3 or 4 large waffles. Their crunchiness is complemented by something cool and smooth like yogurt and, or course, maple syrup, which should be warmed.

OLD-FASHIONED CREAM SCONES

When you taste these you begin to understand one reason why, in the British Isles, the ritual of tea pre-empted all other activities. We don't encounter them very often in this country, which is our loss as they are sumptuously good, delicate and rich. They must be light, for which the gentlest handling is necessary. Scones are related to our biscuits, but these have an almost cakey, rather than flaky, texture. Like English muffins, they may be cooked on top of the stove.

Preheat oven to 450°F. Sift together, into a mixing bowl, the flour, baking powder, and salt. Add the butter in small chunks and cut it into the flour with a pastry blender or two knives until the mixture is like small peas.

In another bowl beat the two eggs. Add honey and cream. Beat again. Pour the liquid into the flour. Toss together lightly with two forks until it's barely mixed. Turn dough out onto a liberally floured surface. It will be quite moist. Dip your hands in flour and have extra flour ready. Gather up the dough and pat gently to hold it together. After a minute or so it should no longer fall apart.

If it does, sprinkle with a little more flour. Fold dough over onto itself; press gently (imagine it is being kneaded by butterflies). Do this just a few times. Try not to overwork the flour. Cut the dough in half; form each half into a ball. With your hands pat out each ball into a circle about ½″ thick. Dip a knife into flour and cut each circle into quarters.

With a spatula lift each quarter onto a buttered baking sheet, treating each piece as if it were a thin-shelled egg. Brush the tops with a glaze of egg beaten with a little cream or milk. Bake about 15 minutes; if they seem much too soft leave them in a few minutes more but don't undo all your sensitive work by letting them reach a point of dryness. They will come out puffed and golden.

Traditionally, scones are baked on a griddle on top of the stove. To do this, cut the rounds into quarters, dust the tops with flour (the bottoms have retained some flour from sitting on the board). Preheat ungreased griddle on a low flame. Place the scones on it. Watch them. When the bottoms are browned and they have risen, turn and brown the other side. The heat should be low so they can cook through without burning. This can take 20-25 minutes. Scones are equally good cooked this way, although the surface is dusty rather than glossy and they are not as puffy.

Scones should be eaten hot. Pull apart with your fingers.

To reheat, wrap lightly in foil and warm in a moderate oven or, better yet, split and toast. They won't be as tender, but you'll have your memories.

Makes 8 scones.

2 cups unbleached white flour

1 tablespoon baking powder

½ teaspoon salt

6 tablespoons cold sweet butter (¾ stick)

2 eggs for the dough, plus 1 for the glaze

2 tablespoons honey

½ cup heavy cream

POSY'S RUSSIAN BLACK BREAD

Be forewarned; this is a lot of work—but worth it. The finished loaf looks and feels as heavy as a log but has a fine grain and surprisingly light texture. There are tantalizing suggestions of several mysterious flavors. Slice thin. Delicious to serve with winter soups and buffet suppers.

⅓ cup cornmeal

¾ cup boiling water

¾ cup cold water

2 tablespoons dry yeast

¼ cup warm water

2 oz. unsweetened chocolate

1 tablespoon soft sweet butter

¾ cup dark molasses

1 tablespoon salt

2 teaspoons sugar

2 teaspoons caraway seeds

1 cup cold mashed potatoes

1-1½ cups whole wheat flour, preferably stone-ground

3-4 cups rye flour, preferably stone-ground

1 cup or less unbleached white flour

1 egg for glaze

In a saucepan add the cornmeal to the boiling water. Stir vigorously until it is thick and smooth. Add the cold water gradually, stirring. Let cool to lukewarm.

In a large mixing bowl combine the yeast with the ¼ cup warm water and a pinch of sugar. Stir and let sit until bubbly.

In a small pan melt the chocolate and butter together on very low heat. Let this cool a bit.

To the yeast add the cornmeal mixture, the chocolate and butter, the molasses, salt, sugar, caraway seeds and mashed potatoes. Beat well. Add 1 cup whole wheat flour and beat about 2 minutes with an electric beater or at least 200 strokes by hand. If you have time, let this sponge sit, covered with a towel, for an hour or so. Don't let it overflow the bowl.

Add 3 cups rye flour and mix. If the dough is too mushy to hold together, add another half cup whole wheat and/or up to a cup more rye.

Turn the dough out onto a board dusted with white flour and begin to knead. It's a heavy, sticky mess, so if you get tired, cover the dough and come back later. Add a little white flour if it stays insistently sticky. It never really loses its clinginess (if it does you've probably added too much flour) but it does finally become somewhat elastic, so keep at it.

Put the dough in a buttered bowl, turn it over to coat all sides. Cover with a damp towel and let it sit in a warm place until doubled in size.

Punch the dough down, turn it out onto the board, knead a few times to press out air bubbles. Cut in half, cover with the towel and let it rest for 10 to 15 minutes.

Shape the two pieces into round balls. Place on a greased baking sheet sprinkled with cornmeal. Cover with the towel and let rise in a warm place until almost doubled in size.

Preheat the oven to 400°F. Glaze the loaves with a whole egg beaten with a little water.

Bake loaves for 10 minutes, reduce heat to 350° and bake for another 25 minutes. Tap the bottom of a loaf to test for doneness; if it sounds hollow, the bread is done.

Cool on a rack.

Makes two loaves.

EROTIC TOMATO RYE BREAD

The adjective would seem to refer to the wheat germ and the purported powers of Vitamin E. But even if it's not therapeutic, this bread is a special experience.

In a large mixing bowl combine the yeast with the warm tomato juice and the honey. Let it sit until foaming.

Add the butter, salt and seeds. Beat. Add 2½ cups of white flour and beat with an electric mixer 2 minutes or at least 200 strokes by hand.

Stir in the wheat germ. Gradually mix in the rye flour and enough additional white flour to make a manageable dough.

Turn the dough out onto a floured board; knead until smooth and elastic. Add a little more white flour if it remains too sticky.

Put the dough in a buttered bowl and turn to coat all sides. Cover with a towel and let rise until it has doubled in bulk.

Punch the dough down, turn it out onto a lightly floured board, knead a few times to press out air bubbles, cut in half, cover and let it rest for ten to fifteen minutes.

Grease a baking sheet and dust with cornmeal. Shape the dough into two round or oval loaves, place on the baking sheet, brush the tops with melted butter, slash with a razor if desired. Let rise, covered with the towel, until almost doubled.

Preheat oven to 350°F. Bake about thirty-five minutes, or until the bottoms of the loaves sound hollow when tapped.

Cool on a rack. Makes two loaves.

1½ tablespoons dry yeast

2 cups warm tomato or clamato juice

2 tablespoons honey

2 tablespoons melted butter

2 teaspoons salt

1 tablespoon caraway seeds

1 tablespoon poppy seeds

3 cups unbleached white flour, approximately

¾-1 cup raw wheat germ

3 cups rye flour, preferably stone-ground

WHOLE WHEAT EGG BREAD

A rich, wholesome bread to comfort the stomach on a cold winter's day.

2 cups warm water

2 tablespoons dry yeast

½ teaspoon sugar or honey

½ cup non-fat dry milk

⅓ cup honey

1 tablespoon salt

¼ cup melted butter or light oil

4 egg yolks

3 cups unbleached white flour

4 cups whole wheat flour, approximately, preferably stone-ground

In a large mixing bowl combine ½ cup of the warm water with the yeast and ½ teaspoon sugar or honey. Let it sit until it froths. Add remaining water, dry milk, honey, salt, oil or butter, egg yolks, and white flour.

Beat at least 2 minutes with an electric mixer or 200 strokes by hand. If you have time, cover the bowl with a towel or plastic wrap and let it sit for 30 minutes to two hours.

Gradually beat in the whole wheat flour until the dough clings together and pulls away from the sides of the bowl. Turn the dough out onto a floured surface and knead until it becomes smooth and elastic. Sprinkle with more flour if it remains too sticky to work with but try to keep the dough on the soft side.

Place the dough in a buttered bowl and turn to coat all sides. Cover with a damp towel and let rise until doubled in bulk.

Punch the dough down, turn out onto a floured surface and knead a few times to press out air pockets. Cut in half, cover and let rise about 10 minutes.

Shape the dough into two oblongs and place in greased, 9 × 5-inch loaf pans. Or shape into rounds and put on baking sheets that have been greased and sprinkled with corn meal. Brush the tops with melted butter. If making round loaves, cut crosses in the tops with a sharp knife.

Let the loaves rise until doubled or almost doubled in size. Bake in oven pre-heated to 350°F. about 35 minutes or until the bottoms sound hollow when tapped.

Cool on racks.

Makes two large loaves.

Optional: About 10 minutes before baking time is up, brush loaves wth a glaze of whole egg beaten with 1 tablespoon milk or water.

FAY'S SPICY BATTER BREAD

●

Light and aromatic, this easy bread contains a surprise step which may keep children silent and watchful (for at least five minutes). Start making it in January because you may find it suits every month of the year.

In a large mixing bowl dissolve the yeast in the warm water with the ½ teaspoon sugar or honey. When bubbly, add honey, milk, salt and oil. Blend spices with white flour and add to yeast mixture. Beat with an electric mixer five to ten minutes or by hand, until you require first aid. The longer the beating, the finer the grain. Stir in raisins and nuts. Slowly add whole wheat flour, stirring by hand or with an electric mixer if yours is a heavy-duty one. The dough should be too stiff to continue beating but too moist and sticky to knead.

Grease two 1-lb. coffee or similar type cans with butter or margarine. Divide dough between the cans. Push it down and smooth the tops, but don't try to make it perfect. Grease the insides of the coffee can lids and put them on the cans. Let the loaves rise until the tops pop off. This is where you enlist the aid of children or other unoccupied people, as watchers. Don't worry if the moment the dough rises above the top is missed. That will produce an appealing mushroom when it bakes. But if the dough has gotten away from you it would be prudent to remove the loaves, reshape and let them rise again.

Preheat the oven to 350°F. Bake about 40 minutes. Be sure there is room enough for the tall loaves to rise a little more in the oven.

Slide the loaf out onto your oven-mitted hand. Thump the bottom for doneness. Don't overcook. Cool for a few minutes in their cans; remove and cool on a wire rack. Serve warm for a snack or have spicy round toast the next day.

Makes two loaves.

1 tablespoon dry yeast
½ cup warm water
½ teaspoon sugar or honey
2 tablespoons honey
1 13 oz. can evaporated milk
1 teaspoon salt
2 tablespoons light oil
3 cups unbleached white flour
¼ teaspoon ginger
1 teaspoon cinnamon
½ teaspoon nutmeg
½ cup raisins
½ cup chopped nuts
1½ cups whole wheat flour

CAROLE'S PRUNE BREAD

Dark and delectable as a mid-winter romance.

¾ cup chopped prunes

¼ cup sherry, Madeira, or orange juice

2 eggs

6 tablespoons (¾ stick) soft butter

⅓ cup honey

¾ cup sour cream

1 teaspoon grated lemon rind

1 teaspoon vanilla

1 cup unbleached white flour

½ cup chopped pecans, optional

1 teaspoon baking powder

1 teaspoon baking soda

2 teaspoons cinnamon

1 teaspoon salt

½ cup whole wheat flour

Marinate the prunes for a few hours or overnight in the sherry, Madeira or juice. Pre-heat the oven to 325°F.

In a mixing bowl beat the eggs until light. Add the butter, honey, sour cream, lemon rind and vanilla. Beat well.

Take out 2 tablespoons of the white flour and toss with the prunes. Mix the prunes and nuts into the batter.

Sift together remaining white flour, baking powder, soda, cinnamon and salt. Mix in the whole wheat flour.

Fold the flour mixture into the liquids, stirring just enough to combine thoroughly. Pour the batter into a buttered and floured loaf pan.

Bake at 325°F. for about 55 minutes. At this point the bread will have the consistency of a moist cake, almost a pudding. Serve warm with whipped cream, ice cream or yogurt. Or continue baking for a total of about 90 minutes and serve as a tea bread. Test for doneness by pushing a finger gently into the top to see if it feels soft but springy.

Cool in pan 10 minutes; remove from pan and cool on wire rack.

Makes one loaf.

February

MILL HOLLOW BREAD

According to her husband, Edith Newlin Chase has been baking (and refining) this bread for 40 years, and they never tire of it. I've been making it for 4 years and look forward to the next 36. It is a resplendent mix of contrasts and complements, yet thoroughly basic. This recipe makes three loaves: one to eat right away, one to freeze for next week's toast, and one to give the first person who wanders within wafting distance.

2 cups milk

3 tablespoons butter, oil or bacon grease

1 tablespoon salt (if using bacon grease reduce salt to 2 teaspoons)

⅔ cup maple syrup (or honey if you don't have access to maple syrup)

2 tablespoons blackstrap molasses

2 tablespoons dry yeast

½ cup warm water

½ teaspoon honey or sugar

4 cups unbleached white flour

½ cup sunflower kernels

¼ cup wheat germ

¼ cup bran flakes

½ cup rye flour, preferably stone-ground

About 3 cups whole wheat flour, preferably stone-ground

In a saucepan scald the milk. Add the butter, oil, or grease, salt, maple syrup and blackstrap molasses. Stir to mix.

Cool to room temperature.

In a large mixing bowl dissolve the yeast in the warm water with the half-teaspoon sugar or honey. When frothy, add the milk mixture and 4 cups white flour. Beat 2 minutes with an electric mixer or at least 200 strokes by hand.

Mix in the sunflower kernels, wheat germ, bran, and rye flour. Gradually add the whole wheat flour until the dough clings together and leaves the sides of the bowl.

Turn the dough out onto a floured surface and knead until smooth and elastic, adding a bit more whole wheat flour if the dough remains obstinately sticky.

Put the dough in a buttered bowl, turn to coat all sides, cover with a damp towel and let rise until it has doubled in bulk.

Punch the dough down, turn out onto a lightly floured surface, knead a few times to press out air bubbles, cut into three equal pieces, cover with the towel and let rest 10 minutes.

Shape the pieces into loaves and place in three medium-sized, greased loaf pans. Brush the tops with melted butter. Cover with towel and let rise again until almost doubled.

Preheat the oven to 350°F. Bake 35 to 40 minutes or until the bottoms sound hollow when tapped. Remove to racks to cool.

Edith Newlin: Cut off the end slice of the least perfect loaf, butter well and serve to yourself with hot tea as the Cook's Treat! Makes three medium loaves.

did not raise well—only tried once

SPOON BREAD

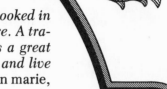

Spoon bread is a moist version of corn bread. It is usually cooked in a casserole or soufflé dish and is close to a pudding in texture. A traditional "special dish" on Southern tables, spoon bread is a great favorite with children and others who can ignore calories and live only for the moment. This version, which is cooked in a bain marie, or water bath, is especially voluptuous.

Pour the boiling water over the cornmeal, stirring briskly. Add the butter and honey and stir until well mixed. Let cool a bit. Preheat the oven to 350°F.

In another bowl beat the eggs until they are light in color and slightly thickened. Add the milk, sprinkle in the salt and baking powder and beat well to mix.

Add a little of the liquid to the cooled cornmeal and mix it in thoroughly. Then add the meal mixture to the liquids and beat until blended.

Pour the batter into a buttered 2-quart casserole or soufflé dish. Put it in a pan of hot water. Water should reach about halfway up the baking dish. Bake at 350°F. for about 1 hour and 15 minutes or until the center feels just set. (A knife blade inserted will come out clean.) As with soufflés, you can cook spoon bread for a shorter or longer time according to how firm you like it.

Serve right away, dipping it from the dish it was cooked in, with a large spoon, hence the name. Offer more butter for those who have no scruples.

This will feed 4 to 6.

1⅓ cups boiling water
1 cup yellow cornmeal, preferably stone-ground
4 tablespoons sweet butter (½ stick)
2 teaspoons honey
3 eggs
1¼ cups milk
1 teaspoon salt
3 teaspoons baking powder

QUICK WINTER HERB BREAD

A provocative encounter between herbs and raisins.
Good with soup.

1½ cups unbleached white
   flour
½ teaspoon salt
1½ teaspoons baking
   powder
½ teaspoon baking soda
¼ teaspoon dried
   marjoram
⅛ teaspoon dried oregano
½ teaspoon dried basil
   pinch dried thyme
½ cup raisins
½ cup chopped nuts
1 egg
2 tablespoons honey
4 tablespoons melted
   sweet butter
¾ cup buttermilk or sour
   milk

more like cake or biscuits

Preheat oven to 400°F.

Sift together the flour, salt, baking powder and soda. Sprinkle in the herbs and toss with two forks until evenly distributed. Mix in the raisins and nuts and toss again, making sure they don't stick together.

In a large mixing bowl beat the egg until it is light and slightly thickened. Add the honey and beat to blend. Beat in the melted butter and buttermilk.

Blend dry and wet ingredients together with just a few strokes. Turn out onto a well-floured board. Using a pastry scraper or egg turner, reach under the dough and lift it up on top of itself. Do this several times and pat the mixture together gently with your floured hands. If it is very gooey, sprinkle on a bit more flour but be stingy. When the dough just holds together but is still lumpy, put it into a buttered cake tin. With lightly floured palms, pat lightly to fill the pan. Bake at 400°F. about 20 minutes or until lightly browned and the middle feels springy when pressed. Don't overcook. Cut into wedges and serve warm with butter.

Serves 8.

Miller filling bags at Baile's Old Mill in North Carolina.

ANADAMA RAISIN BATTER BREAD

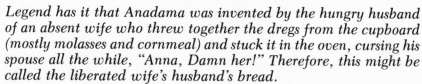

Legend has it that Anadama was invented by the hungry husband of an absent wife who threw together the dregs from the cupboard (mostly molasses and cornmeal) and stuck it in the oven, cursing his spouse all the while, "Anna, Damn her!" Therefore, this might be called the liberated wife's husband's bread.

This version would be especially suited to the desperate husband since it requires no kneading. Cornmeal and molasses proved to be a fortuitous combination, here enhanced with raisins. The crusty coarseness of a batter bread is also appropriate to the legend. Curses will die with the first whiff from the oven, and lucky is the man who can slice off the end while still warm and butter it all for himself. If wife comes home she may be persuaded to stay around for a while. And let her husband do more of the cooking.

In a good-sized saucepan bring the milk and 1 cup water to a boil. Turn off the heat and sprinkle in the corn meal, stirring energetically with a wire whisk or fork. Add the butter and molasses and stir until evenly mixed. Cool to lukewarm.

In a large mixing bowl dissolve the yeast in the half-cup warm water with the sugar or honey. When bubbly, add cornmeal mixture, salt, and 2½ cups of the flour. It should be thick but still beatable. Beat 5 minutes with an electric mixer.

Stir in the raisins. Gradually add 2½ to 3 cups more flour, beating with a large spoon until the batter is too stiff to continue beating and holds together in a mass in the center of the bowl.

Cover the bowl with a damp towel and let it sit until the dough has risen to twice its original volume. Stir down with the spoon. If you wish, let it rise a second time. Stir down. Divide the dough between two buttered large loaf pans. Be sure you get equal amounts in each pan. Squish it into the corners with your fingers. Press to smooth the tops a bit; don't worry if they look like a lava flow.

Cover the pans with a towel and let rise until batter reaches the tops of the pans. Preheat oven to 350°F. Bake 40 to 45 minutes, until the loaves are brown but don't quite have a hollow sound when tapped on the bottoms. Remove them from the pans and put directly on the oven rack. Bake another 5 minutes to crisp the crust.

Cool on a rack. Now you have something better to put in the cupboard than what you took out of it.

1 cup milk

1 cup water

1 cup corn meal, preferably yellow and stone-ground

3 tablespoons sweet butter

½ cup unsulphured molasses

½ cup warm water

2 tablespoons dry yeast

½ teaspoon sugar or honey

2 teaspoons salt

5½ (approximate) cups unbleached white flour

1 cup gold raisins

DARK RYE BREAD

Tender, fragrant and subtly spicy.

2 tablespoons dry yeast

2 cups warm water

½ teaspoon sugar or honey

¼ cup blackstrap molasses

¼ cup maple syrup
(or 2 tablespoons honey
and 2 tablespoons
unsulphured molasses)

¼ cup soft sweet butter
(½ stick)

1 tablespoon salt

2 tablespoons cocoa

1 tablespoon caraway
seeds

3-4 cups unbleached white
flour

3 cups rye flour,
preferably
stone-ground

Cornmeal

In a large mixing bowl dissolve the yeast in the warm water with the half teaspoon sugar or honey. Let it sit until bubbly.

Add the blackstrap molasses, maple syrup, soft butter, salt, cocoa and caraway seeds and beat well.

Add 3 cups of the white flour and beat 2 minutes with an electric mixer or at least 200 strokes by hand.

Add the 3 cups rye flour and mix until the dough leaves the sides of the bowl.

Turn the dough out onto a floured board and knead until it is smooth and elastic. Sprinkle with a little more white flour if it remains too sticky to handle. When it becomes elastic, stop kneading even if it remains a little clingy to your fingers.

Put the dough in a buttered bowl, turn to coat all sides. Cover with a damp towel and let rise until doubled in bulk.

Punch the dough down, turn it out onto the board, knead a few times to press out air bubbles, cut in half, cover with the towel and let rest 10 to 15 minutes.

Shape the dough into two round or oval loaves and put on a greased baking sheet which has been dusted with cornmeal. You may cut a cross or other design in the tops with a sharp knife. Brush the tops of the loaves with melted butter, cover with the towel and let rise in a warm place until almost doubled in size.

Preheat oven to 375°F. Bake 35 to 40 minutes, or until the bottoms sound hollow when tapped. Cool on a rack.

Makes two loaves.

WHEAT GERM BUTTERMILK PANCAKES

A lovely combination of maple and buttermilk flavors with a slight wheat germ crunchiness. Serve with more maple syrup.

1¼ cups unbleached white
flour

1 teaspoon baking soda

½ teaspoon salt

¼ cup wheat germ

2 eggs

6 tablespoons melted
butter

2 tablespoons maple syrup
(or honey)

2 cups buttermilk

Sift together the flour, soda and salt. Stir in the wheat germ. Set aside. Beat the eggs until they are light in color and thickened.

Beat the melted butter (not too hot), maple syrup and buttermilk into the eggs. Add the flour mixture and beat enough to mix well. Preheat a griddle or large heavy skillet to medium hot and grease lightly with oil.

Drop the batter onto the griddle about 2 tablespoons at a time. The pancakes should be small. Cook until brown on the bottom, then turn and brown the other side. The outside should be crisp and the inside remain tender. You probably won't have to re-grease the griddle between batches.

Serve right off the griddle if possible or keep warm on a platter in a low oven.

This makes about 3 dozen pancakes.

PALACSINTA
(Hungarian Crepes)

In my New York years, late at night we would creep into a diminutive restaurant on Manhattan's Upper West Side to perform gluttony on palacsinta (with—oh!—choice of fillings) and cups of very dark, rich hot chocolate. In dead of winter it was (perhaps is) the indulgence of last resort.

Sift together the flour and salt. Set aside. In a large bowl beat the eggs and yolk until very light and frothy. Add the milk, water, honey and melted butter and beat to mix. Beat in the flour. Batter will be thin.

Take a crepe pan or heavy small skillet with sloping slides. The bottom should be between 5 inches and 6 inches in diameter. Using a pastry brush, grease lightly with a few drops vegetable oil. Preheat over medium hot unit. With one hand in an oven mitt, hold the handle of the pan. With the other hand pour a small quantity of batter into the pan (about 3 tablespoons), as you simultaneously tilt the pan to and fro so the batter covers the bottom. The purpose of this procedure is to produce a pancake which is as thin as possible. Since the batter begins to cook as soon as it hits the pan, it will not spread evenly over the bottom unless you tilt the pan. Practice on the first few until you discover exactly how little batter you need to cover the bottom. The less the batter the finer the palacsinta! Cook the pancake until it is golden brown on the bottom. This doesn't take long. Gently lift an edge with a fork to see how it's doing. With the aid of the fork, lift the edge and slide an egg turner under the pancake to flip it. Cook to golden brown and crisp on the other side. It should not be necessary to grease the pan after the first pancake. Keep them warm in a low oven while you do the rest.

Fill the palacsinta with any of the following:

Plain yogurt mixed with a little honey
Applesauce and raisins
Apple filling from Norwegian Apple Pancakes (see page 181).
Apricot jam heated with a little orange liquor or rum
Ricotta cheese with gold raisins or chopped nuts or both
Anything else which sparks your imagination

Fold the ends over the filling and turn the palacsinta so the open edge is down. Sprinkle with sugar or cinnamon sugar and very thinly slivered almonds.

This recipe makes 18-20 palacsintas. Two per person is about right, to satisfy hunger if not desire.

1¼ cups unbleached white flour
⅛ teaspoon salt
2 eggs plus one egg yolk
¾ cup milk
¾ cup water
1 tablespoon honey
2 tablespoons melted sweet butter

Standing outside his bakery shop in Chester, Vt., John McLure displays the French loaves he has baked. Inside the shop he shows the loaves just ready for the oven.

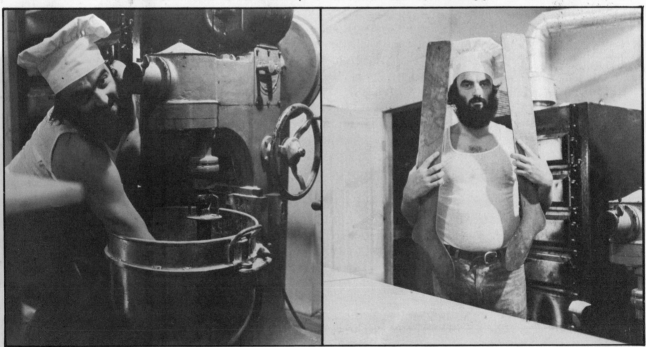

For making bread for many customers, John needs this enormous dough mixer (left). The old stocking forms he holds (right) are for sliding the French loaves into the oven.

FRENCH BREAD
WITH BEER

*An elusive tang permeates this loaf. Don't worry; the alcohol
evaporates during baking so there's no need to request I.D.'s.*

Heat the beer or ale until it is warm (not hot), pour into a large
mixing bowl, add the honey and yeast, stir and let sit until the yeast
is dissolved and bubbling.

Add the syrup, oil, salt and white flour and beat 2 minutes
with an electric mixer or at least 200 strokes by hand.

Add, gradually, about 2 cups whole wheat flour, or as much as
it takes to make a dough that pulls away from the sides of the bowl
and holds together.

Turn the dough out onto a floured board and knead until it is
smooth and elastic. Sprinkle on a little more whole wheat flour if it
remains too sticky.

Put the dough into a buttered bowl, turn to coat all sides,
cover and let it rise until it has doubled in bulk.

Punch the dough down, turn it out onto a lightly floured
board, knead a few times to press out air bubbles, cut in half, cover
with the towel and let it rest 10 to 15 minutes.

Butter a large baking sheet and dust with cornmeal. Take each
ball of dough and, with a rolling pin, roll out into a rectangle. Roll
up each rectangle, along the long axis, like a tight jelly roll. Pinch
the ends together to seal them and tuck them under slightly. Carefully place the rolls on the baking sheet, seam side down. Make several diagonal slashes along the top of each loaf with a razor blade or
sharp knife. Brush the tops with melted butter, cover with a towel
and let them rise until almost doubled.

Preheat the oven to 450°F. Just before the loaves go into the
oven, spray them with cold water from a clean plant mister or other
spray bottle (or brush with a pastry brush). Put the loaves in the
oven, throw a small amount of water onto the hot oven floor to
create a cloud of steam and quickly shut the door. Repeat spraying
the loaves and throwing water on the floor after five minutes. (If
you don't want to throw water in the oven, place a shallow pan of
boiling water on oven bottom before baking.)

After 10 minutes, repeat spraying and turn the heat down to
375°. Leave in oven another 15 minutes, or until the loaves sound
hollow when tapped on the bottom. Baking time is about 25 minutes in all. Cool on a rack.

Makes two long loaves.

1½ cups (1 12-oz. can) beer
    or ale
1 tablespoon dry yeast
1 tablespoon honey
1 tablespoon malt syrup or
    maple syrup
2 tablespoons light oil
2 teaspoons salt
2 cups unbleached white
    flour
2 cups whole wheat flour,
    preferably stone-ground
    Cornmeal

APRICOT QUICK BREAD

This makes a golden, fragrant loaf, a pleasing combination of tartness and sweetness.

Preheat oven to 350°F.

Pour the boiling water over the apricots, enough to cover them, and let them steep about 10 minutes. Drain and chop the apricots.

In a large mixing bowl beat the egg until light and slightly thick, add the honey, melted butter or oil, apricot nectar and orange juice, orange peel and vanilla. Beat well. Stir in the apricots and nuts.

Sift together the flour, baking powder, soda, salt and ginger.

Fold the flour mixture into the liquids, stirring just enough to mix thoroughly.

Pour the batter into a greased loaf pan and bake about an hour, or until the top is springy to the touch.

Cool loaf in pan for 10-15 minutes before removing to cool on a rack.

Makes 1 loaf.

1 cup dried apricots
  boiling water
1 egg
⅔ cup honey
2 tablespoons melted butter
  or oil
1 6-oz. can apricot nectar
  plus enough orange juice
  to make 1 cup (if apricot
  nectar is not available,
  use all orange juice)
  grated peel of 1 orange
1 teaspoon vanilla
½ cup chopped nuts
2 cups unbleached white
  flour
2 teaspoons baking powder
1 teaspoon baking soda
1 teaspoon salt
¼ teaspoon ginger

5-1-13 Revisions

1 c chopped apricots
½ c chopped Raisins
½ c chopped nuts
¼ c applesauce
1 t vanilla
1 t orange extract
⅔ c Honey   1 c white
1 c juice (any) 1 c whole wheat
1 T baking Powder
2 t " Soda
1 t Salt
1 t ginger

Edith Chase mans the sifter and keeps a watchful eye on her husband Herman Chase turning the dough mixer.

SOUR CREAM PECAN COFFEECAKE

Moist and crunchy, this coffeecake is best warm from the oven. Two of its three parts can be mixed the night before so with a minimum of effort you can produce something luxurious to take the curse off a dark winter's breakfast.

Sift together flour, salt, baking powder and soda. Cover. Set aside.

Combine brown sugar and cinnamon in a flat-bottomed bowl. Blend with a fork. Cut butter into small chunks and cut into sugar mixture with a pastry blender. Mixture should resemble small peas. Add the chopped nuts and toss with a fork to mix. Cover with plastic wrap and refrigerate until time to use.

When ready to put cake together, preheat oven to 375°F. In large mixing bowl beat the egg until light and somewhat thickened. Add vanilla, maple syrup, sour cream and milk. Beat thoroughly. (If using honey add first and beat separately to mix.) Gently fold egg and flour mixtures together, stirring until almost blended. Pour one-half of batter into a buttered eight or nine inch square baking dish. Sprinkle half of topping over surface. Cover with remaining half of batter, then sprinkle on the rest of the topping. Bake 30 to 35 minutes or until middle is set. Don't overcook. It should be moist but not doughy.

Part I

1½ cups unbleached white flour

½ teaspoon salt

1 teaspoon baking powder

½ teaspoon baking soda

Part II (Topping)

¾ cup brown sugar (packed)

1 tablespoon flour

1½ teaspoons cinnamon

4 tablespoons sweet butter, slightly softened

1 cup finely chopped pecans or walnuts

Part III

1 egg

1 teaspoon vanilla

¼ cup maple syrup (if unavailable use honey)

½ cup sour cream

¼ cup milk

CZECH RAISIN BRAID

Lovely to look at, fun to create, and nice to eat if you can bear to put a knife to it.

1 cup milk

6 tablespoons sweet butter (¾ stick)

⅓ cup honey

1 teaspoon salt

1 tablespoon dry yeast (plus 1 teaspoon if you're in a hurry)

¼ cup warm water

½ teaspoon sugar or honey

¼ teaspoon ginger grated rind of 1 lemon and 1 orange

2 eggs

5-5½ cups unbleached white flour

¾-1 cup gold raisins

1 egg for glaze Slivered almonds (optional)

Scald the milk in a saucepan, add the butter, honey and salt, and let sit until lukewarm. In a large mixing bowl combine the yeast, warm water and half-teaspoon sugar or honey. When bubbly, add the milk mixture, ginger, grated rind, and eggs.

Beat thoroughly. Add 2½ cups of the flour and beat at least 200 strokes by hand or two minutes with an electric mixer. Stir in the raisins. Gradually add about 2½ cups more flour or enough to make a dough that pulls away from the sides of the bowl.

Turn the dough out onto a floured board and knead until smooth and elastic, adding more flour as necessary. Put the dough into a buttered bowl, turn to grease all sides. Cover with a towel and let rise until doubled in bulk.

Punch the dough down, turn out onto a lightly floured board, knead a few times to press out air bubbles, cut in half, cover and let rest about 10 minutes. Wrap one half in the towel and set aside. Take the other half and divide into three equal pieces. Roll out each piece with your hands into a long rope (the length will depend on your energy and the size of your baking sheet—the finished braid must fit onto the sheet with room to spare for expanding).

Braid the three ropes, twisting the ends underneath slightly and pinching them together to seal them. Carefully lift the braid and place it on a large, buttered cookie sheet or jelly roll pan; place it diagonally if there is any question of crowding.

Take the second piece of dough and divide it so that there is about ⅔ in one part and ⅓ in the other. Wrap the smaller piece in the towel, set aside. Divide the larger piece into three equal parts. Make a second braid, just as you did the first, remembering to seal the ends.

You now have a second, smaller braid. Place it on top of the original braid, centering it. Form a third braid out of the remaining piece of dough and place this small braid on top of the second one. You now have a pyramid of three braids in graduated sizes. Make sure they are stable and centered or the whole construction may become alarmingly lopsided as it rises and bakes.

Brush the braid with melted butter, being sure to get some into all the crooks and crannies. Cover with a light cloth and let rise until not quite doubled. Meanwhile pre-heat the oven to 350°F.

Bake about 45 minutes, remove from the oven and brush all over with a glaze of whole egg beaten with 2 tablespoons water. Sprinkle with slivered almonds if desired. Return to the oven for 5-10 minutes longer. This bread is a hard one to test for doneness; try thunking the sides for crustiness or poking a cake tester into a crevice.

Be sure you will not be diverted before slipping a large pancake turner under each end of the braid and lifting to a rack to cool.

Makes one large loaf.

P.S. If you're not feeling sculptural this day, skip the multiple braiding, divide the dough in half, and shape into two braided loaves. Reduce baking time to about 35 to 40 minutes.

March

HOT CROSS BUNS

These traditional Easter rolls, plump and spicy, should be an ecumenical delicacy.

½ cup milk

½ cup sweet butter
(1 stick)

⅓ cup honey

¾ cup mashed potatoes
(use instant if you must)

1½ tablespoons dry yeast

½ cup warm water

½ teaspoon sugar or honey

2 eggs

1½ teaspoons salt

1 teaspoon cinnamon

½ teaspoon nutmeg

¼ teaspoon ground cloves

5 cups unbleached white
flour, approximately

⅔ cup currants

¼ cup diced candied
orange peel, optional

Bee Hive

In a saucepan scald the milk. Add the butter, honey and mashed potatoes. Stir with a wire whisk or fork until the mixture is smooth and the butter melted. Cool to lukewarm.

In a large mixing bowl, dissolve the yeast in the warm water with the half teaspoon sugar or honey. When it is bubbling, add the cooled milk mixture, eggs, salt, spices and 2 cups of the flour. Beat with an electric mixer 2 minutes or at least 200 strokes by hand. Add the currants and peel. Gradually add about 3 cups more flour, or enough to make a dough that clings together and leaves the sides of the bowl. Turn the dough out onto a floured board and knead until smooth and elastic, adding a little more flour if the dough remains sticky. Try to keep the dough on the soft side. Put the dough in a buttered bowl and turn it over to coat all sides. Cover with a towel and let rise until doubled in bulk. Punch the dough down, turn it out onto a lightly floured board and knead a few times to press out air bubbles. Cut the dough into 24 equal pieces each about the size of a large egg. Cover with a towel and let rest for 10 to 15 minutes. Form each piece of dough into a smooth ball by rolling between your palms. Tuck any edges under and pinch to seal, leaving a smooth round surface on top. Place the balls on buttered baking sheets, leaving enough room between them for expansion. (If you don't have enough baking sheets, refrigerate the rest of the dough for later use.) Brush the tops with melted butter and let rise, covered with a light cloth, until not quite double in size. Keep watch; the texture of these buns suffers from over-rising.

Meanwhile preheat the oven to 375°F. or put the shaped buns on baking sheets, covered with a damp towel, in the refrigerator to rise overnight, so you can have them piping hot for breakfast. If they haven't risen quite enough by the next morning, put them on top of the stove while you preheat the oven. Brush the tops again with melted butter. Bake about 20 minutes; break one open to test for doneness.

Best warm from the oven, but cool on a rack if not serving immediately. They can be re-heated in a moderate oven, wrapped loosely in foil. If you wish to glaze them, which is done most successfully when they are cool, make a paste of confectioners' sugar, a little almond flavoring or grated lemon peel, and just enough water, milk or orange juice to make a thick icing. Brush this over the tops of the buns or, as is traditional, dribble it on in the form of a cross. A cross may also be cut into each bun with a sharp knife before the final rising, then accentuated with frosting after baking. Or brush warm buns with butter and dust with cinnamon sugar.

Makes about 24 buns.

MAPLE APPLESAUCE QUICK BREAD

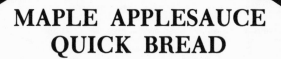

It's hard to know whether to make this when the maple syrup is fresh from the sugar house or when you've just simmered up some applesauce from a basket of windfalls. Fortunately, each will keep into the other's season. And don't be deterred if you have to use store-bought applesauce; the bread will still be moist and spicy.

Preheat the oven to 350°F.

In a large mixing bowl beat the eggs until they are light and slightly thickened. Add the maple syrup, melted butter and apple-sauce and beat again. Stir in the nuts.

Sift together the flour, baking powder, soda, salt, cinnamon, mace and nutmeg. Stir in the wheat germ with a fork until evenly distributed.

Add the flour to the liquid ingredients and fold in gently until just mixed.

If you are using homemade applesauce which is quite thick, the batter may be on the stiff side. In this case, stir in 2 tablespoons to ¼ cup buttermilk or milk.

Pour the batter into a buttered, large loaf pan or casserole. Bake about 50 to 55 minutes or until the top feels springy when pressed with your finger. Cool in the pan for 10 minutes. Remove to cool on a rack.

Makes one large loaf.

2 eggs
⅓ cup maple syrup
⅓ cup melted sweet butter or light oil
1½ cups applesauce
¾ cup chopped nuts
2 cups unbleached white flour
2 teaspoons baking powder
½ teaspoon baking soda
½ teaspoon salt
1 teaspoon cinnamon
½ teaspoon mace
¼ teaspoon ground nutmeg
¼ cup raw wheat germ

French bread power

MRS. SMITH'S ZESTY WHOLE WHEAT SOURDOUGH FRENCH BREAD

This bread got rave reviews from a sailboat picnic, but it also passes the landlocked test: crusty and individualistic, yet amiable and not too sour. Have an indoor picnic with a bowl of soup, some cheeses or a strongly seasoned omelet.

In a glass or pottery bowl mix together the starter, 1 cup each white and whole wheat flour, 1 cup warm water and 1 tablespoon honey. Cover with plastic wrap and let sit in a warm, draft-free place overnight or up to 24 hours.

In a large mixing bowl dissolve the yeast in the half-cup water with the honey. When bubbly, add the starter mixture, salt and white flour and beat thoroughly, 2 minutes with an electric mixer or at least 200 strokes by hand. Mix in the wheat germ.

Gradually add enough whole wheat flour to make a dough that clings together and leaves the sides of the bowl. Turn the dough out onto a floured board and knead until smooth and elastic, sprinkling with a little more whole wheat flour as necessary if it remains too sticky. Place the dough in a buttered bowl, turn to coat all sides, cover with a damp towel and let rise until doubled in bulk. Punch the dough down and, if you have time, let it rise again in the bowl. Punch the dough down again, turn it out onto a lightly floured board, knead a few times, cut in half, cover, let rest 10 minutes.

Roll out one half of the dough with a rolling pin into a long rectangle. Starting with a long side, roll into a tight tube. Tuck the ends under, pinch them to seal and place, seam side down, on a greased baking sheet which has been dusted with corn meal. Repeat with the other piece of dough. With a sharp knife slash the tops of the loaves in long diagonals. Brush the tops with melted butter, cover with a light cloth and let rise until not quite doubled in size. Preheat the oven to 400°F. Place a shallow pan of boiling water on the bottom of the oven. Using a clean plant mister or other spray bottle, spray loaves with cold water. Put in oven immediately. Bake 5 minutes, remove and spray loaves again with cold water. Return to oven. Repeat after another five minutes. Remove the pan of water and continue baking 15 to 20 minutes more (25 to 30 minutes in all) or until the bottoms of the loaves sound hollow when tapped. Cool loaves on a rack.

Makes two loaves.

1 cup sourdough starter
1 cup unbleached white flour
1 cup whole wheat flour, preferably stone-ground
1 cup warm water
1 tablespoon honey
½ tablespoon dry yeast
½ cup warm water
1 tablespoon honey
2 teaspoons salt
1 cup unbleached white flour
⅓ cup raw wheat germ
2 cups whole wheat flour, approximately

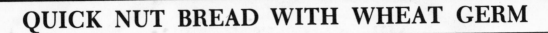

QUICK NUT BREAD WITH WHEAT GERM

This is moist, crunchy and quite rich.

1 egg
⅓ cup honey
¼ cup melted butter (½ stick)
½ cup buttermilk or sour milk
¼ teaspoon almond extract
¼ teaspoon vanilla
½ cup slivered almonds
½ cup ground walnuts or pecans
1 cup unbleached white flour
1½ teaspoons baking powder
½ teaspoon baking soda
1 teaspoon salt
¼ cup wheat germ

Preheat the oven to 350°F. In a large mixing bowl beat the egg; add the honey, melted butter, buttermilk, almond extract and vanilla. Beat again. Stir in the nuts. Sift together the flour, baking powder, soda and salt. Mix in the wheat germ. Combine wet and dry ingredients, stirring just enough to mix thoroughly. Pour into a medium size (8 × 4 × 2½ inches) buttered loaf pan. Bake about 45 minutes or until center feels springy when pressed with your finger. Cool bread in pan 10 minutes. Remove and cool on wire rack.

Makes 1 loaf.

CORNMEAL WHEAT GERM MUFFINS

1⅓ cup unbleached white flour
3 teaspoons baking powder
½ teaspoon salt
¾ cup cornmeal, preferably stone-ground
¼ cup wheat germ
2 eggs
¼ cup maple syrup (preferably) or honey
½ cup heavy cream

Preheat the oven to 400°F.

Sift together the flour, baking powder and salt. Mix in the cornmeal and wheat germ with a fork.

In another bowl beat the eggs until light in color and slightly thickened. Beat in the maple syrup and cream. Add the dry ingredients and fold in with a rubber spatula or wooden spoon. Stop before the flour mixture is thoroughly incorporated and while the batter is still rough and lumpy.

Spoon the batter into buttered muffin tins, filling each one about ⅔ full.

Bake about 15 minutes.

Makes 12 medium muffins.

excellent

TRITICALE BREAD

Triticale flour may be the wave of the future. A hybrid of wheat and rye, it has been called the first man-made cereal grain. Although developed in the late 19th century, only recently has it begun to be grown in any volume in the United States. Its star quality is its high protein content (one-third more than whole wheat). It's also nice to work with and has a lovely flavor.

In a saucepan scald the milk and add the butter, honey, molasses and salt. Cool to lukewarm.

In a large mixing bowl dissolve the yeast in the warm water with the teaspoon sugar or honey. When bubbly, add the milk mixture, egg, and 3 cups white flour and beat at least 2 minutes with an electric mixer or at least 200 strokes by hand.

Mix in the sunflower kernels. Gradually add the triticale flour, as much as it takes to make a dough that clings together and leaves the sides of the bowl.

Turn the dough out onto a floured surface and knead until smooth and elastic, adding a little more triticale flour if the dough remains persistently sticky. Be patient and try not to add more than necessary—given time it will become more pliant. Place the dough in a buttered bowl, turn over to coat all sides. Cover with a towel and let rise until doubled in bulk.

Punch the dough down, turn it out onto a lightly floured surface, knead a few times to press out air bubbles, divide in half, cover with the towel, and let rest for about 10 minutes.

Form the lumps into oblongs and place them in two buttered medium to large loaf pans. Brush the tops with melted butter and let rise again, covered with the towel, until almost doubled.

Preheat the oven to 350°F. Bake about 40 minutes, or until the bottoms of the loaves sound hollow when tapped. Remove loaves from the pans and cool on a rack.

Makes two loaves.

1 cup milk

¼ cup sweet butter (½ stick)

¼ cup honey

¼ cup unsulphured molasses

2 teaspoons salt

2 tablespoons dry yeast

1 cup warm water

1 teaspoon honey or sugar

1 egg

3 cups unbleached white flour

⅔ cup sunflower kernels

3½ cups triticale flour, approximately

RICH WHITE BATTER BREAD

Very easy and slightly reminiscent of salt rising bread. This pungent loaf makes excellent toast.

1½ cups milk
  2 tablespoons sweet butter
  2 tablespoons honey
¼ teaspoon ground ginger
  2 teaspoons salt
  2 tablespoons dry yeast
½ cup warm water
  1 teaspoon sugar or honey
  4 eggs
  6 cups unbleached white
    flour

really good
not too good
for communion bread

In a saucepan scald the milk; add butter, 2 tablespoons honey, ginger and salt. Cool.

In a large bowl dissolve the yeast in the warm water with the sugar or honey. When this is bubbly, add cooled milk mixture. Add eggs, one at a time, beating well after each.

Add 3 cups of the flour and beat thoroughly for at least 5 minutes with electric mixer. (A finer texture will result if you can let this sponge sit, covered with a towel, for an hour or so.) Beat in 3 more cups flour or enough to form a mass which clings together, leaving the sides of the bowl. You may have to resort to a wooden spoon at this point.

Cover and let dough rise in its bowl until it has doubled in bulk. Stir down with a wooden spoon and divide equally between two 9 × 5-inch buttered loaf pans. You may feel like you are pulling taffy but don't give up. Smooth the dough out as best you can with the spoon or your hands. Cover and let the dough rise until it reaches the tops of the pans. Preheat oven to 375°F. Bake 25 to 30 minutes or until the loaves sound hollow when tapped on the bottom. Remove from the pans and put directly on the oven rack for another couple of minutes baking.

Makes 2 large loaves.

Antique bread board.

RAISED BUCKWHEAT PANCAKES

●

An incubation period lightens the buckwheat flour and tames its slightly odd flavor to a statement rather than an overstatement.

These are breakfast pancakes and should be started the night before (or they could be supper pancakes, in which case start them in the morning).

Scald the milk, add 2 tablespoons butter and honey. Cool to lukewarm. In a large bowl combine yeast, warm water and half-teaspoon sugar. Mix together the white and buckwheat flours and salt. When the yeast is bubbling, add the cooled milk mixture and flours. Stir thoroughly. Cover with plastic and let sit several hours or overnight.

When ready to cook, beat the eggs until light, add the maple syrup and ½ cup melted butter. Sprinkle baking powder over the top and beat in. Combine with the buckwheat mixture and mix well.

Preheat a griddle or large heavy skillet to moderately hot. Grease lightly. Drop the batter onto the griddle, about 2 tablespoons at a time, to make small cakes. Fry until crisp and brown on one side, turn and cook briefly.

You may not have to re-grease the griddle between batches. Serve at once as they will toughen if they sit around. Sweet butter, maple syrup and plain yogurt seem to be the perfect accompaniment.

This amount makes about 4 dozen small pancakes. If you wish to halve the recipe use 1 whole egg and 1 egg white.

1 cup milk
2 tablespoons sweet butter
2 tablespoons honey
¾ cup warm water
2 teaspoons dry yeast
½ teaspoon sugar
½ cup unbleached white flour
1½ cups buckwheat flour
½ teaspoon salt
3 eggs
½ cup melted sweet butter
¼ cup maple syrup
1 teaspoon baking powder

Individual pieces of dough are weighed before being shaped into round loaves at Moravian Bakery.

MORAVIAN SUGAR CAKE

Austere and disciplined societies often have their occasions of sybaritic excess. This lush coffeecake must have been one in the early Moravian settlements of Pennsylvania and North Carolina. This version, which contains practically everything good and fattening from the baker's pantry, is still sweetly outrageous within a contemporary discipline that knows what evil lurks in calories and cholesterol. Though rare, such moments of imprudent pleasure may have their own necessity.

Cook 2 medium potatoes in 1½ cups water. Reserve 1 cup potato water. Mash potatoes. Set aside. In a large saucepan heat the potato water with the butter and lard until the two are melted. Add the honey, mashed potatoes and salt. Mix well with a wire whisk or fork. Cool to lukewarm.

In a large mixing bowl combine the ¼ cup warm water, yeast and ½ teaspoon sugar or honey. Let it sit until bubbly. Add the eggs and potato water mixture. Beat to mix. Add 2½ cups of the flour and beat 2 minutes with an electric mixer or at least 200 strokes by hand. Gradually add more flour until the dough clings together and leaves the sides of the bowl. Turn it out onto a floured board and knead until smooth and elastic, adding a little more flour if the dough remains too sticky. Try to maintain a soft dough.

Put the dough in a buttered bowl, turn to coat all sides. Cover with a towel and let rise until doubled in bulk.

Punch the dough down, turn out onto a lightly floured board, knead a few times, cover and let rise about 10 minutes. Pat or roll the dough out to fit a large shallow baking pan or casserole; lacking that, use several cake pans. Dough should be not more than ½ inch thick. Butter the pans and place the flattened dough in them. Brush the tops with melted butter. Cover with towels and let rise until not quite doubled. With your thumb or a spoon punch craters all over the surface of the dough and fill them with bits of sweet butter. Sprinkle lightly with cinnamon and liberally with brown sugar. Dribble heavy cream over all.

Bake in preheated 400°F. oven 15 to 20 minutes or until golden brown and a toothpick inserted between craters comes out clean. Serve warm from the pan.

To freeze, wrap tightly in foil and place in freezer. When ready to use, leave wrapped in foil and heat in a moderate oven.

Makes 2 large or 3 medium sugar cakes.

1 cup mashed potatoes (about two medium potatoes)
1 cup potato water (in which potatoes were cooked)
⅓ cup sweet butter
⅓ cup lard
⅓ cup honey
1½ teaspoons salt
¼ cup warm water
1½ tablespoons dry yeast
½ teaspoon sugar or honey
2 eggs
6½ cups unbleached white flour approximately

For topping:
sweet butter, brown sugar, cinnamon and heavy cream

SAN FRANCISCO FIREHOUSE BREAD

½ cup minced onion

3 tablespoons sweet butter or light oil

1 13-oz. can evaporated milk

½ cup snipped parsley

2 tablespoons honey

2 teaspoons salt

½ teaspoon dried dillweed or 2 teaspoons chopped fresh dill

¼ teaspoon ground sage

2 tablespoons dry yeast

½ cup warm water

½ teaspoon honey or sugar

4 cups whole wheat flour, preferably stone-ground, or part whole wheat and part unbleached white flour if you prefer

¾ cup cornmeal, preferably stone-ground

Sauté the onion in the butter until it is tender but not browned. Combine onion with the milk, parsley, honey, salt, dill and sage.

In a large mixing bowl combine the yeast, warm water, and the half-teaspoon honey or sugar. When bubbly, mix in the milk mixture. Add 2½ cups flour and beat 2 minutes with an electric mixer or at least 200 strokes by hand. Add the cornmeal and mix thoroughly. Gradually add about 1½ cups more flour, or enough to form a dough that clings together and pulls away from the sides of the bowl.

Turn the dough out onto a floured surface and knead until smooth and elastic, sprinkling with a little more flour if it remains too sticky. Place the dough in a buttered bowl and turn to coat all sides. Cover with a damp towel and let rise until doubled in bulk. Punch the dough down, turn it out onto a lightly floured surface, knead a few times to press out air bubbles, cut in half, cover with the towel and let rest about 10 minutes. Butter well two 1-lb. coffee cans or pans of similar capacity, or butter a baking sheet and sprinkle with cornmeal. Shape the dough into round balls that will fit into the coffee cans. If you are using a baking sheet, they can be any shape. Carefully drop the balls into the coffee cans or place on the sheet. Brush the tops with melted butter. In the case of free-form loaves you may want to slash a cross in the tops with a sharp knife. Cover the loaves with a damp towel and let rise until almost doubled in bulk.

Preheat the oven to 350°F. Bake about 45 minutes, or until the bottoms sound hollow when thumped. Remove from pans to cool on a rack.

Makes two loaves.

AGGIE'S IRISH SODA BREAD

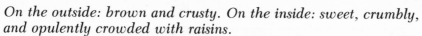

On the outside: brown and crusty. On the inside: sweet, crumbly, and opulently crowded with raisins.

Serve it for breakfast or supper with a pot of fresh sweet butter. And serve it to a lot of people so you won't eat it all yourself.

Preheat oven to 350°F.

Sift the flour, baking powder, soda and salt into a large mixing bowl. Cut the butter into small pieces and add. Cut it into the flour with a pastry blender until the mixture is the size of peas. Add the raisins and toss to distribute evenly, using two forks.

Beat the egg in another bowl until very frothy. Beat in the honey. When it is well blended, beat in the buttermilk.

Gradually pour the liquids into the flour, tossing all the while with a fork so the mixture gets evenly moistened. Continue tossing lightly with two forks until the batter comes together; it doesn't have to be completely mixed and should be very rough and lumpy.

Butter a heavy skillet or casserole, 10 to 11 inches in diameter and 2 to 3 inches deep. Round is the traditional shape. Spoon batter out into the pan and push it gently to fill the pan. It can mound up somewhat in the middle. Bake at 350°F. about an hour or until the middle is set. Cut out a piece to test if necessary.

Cut into wedges and serve warm from the pan.

Serves 12, more or less.

- 3 cups unbleached white flour
- 2 teaspoons baking powder
- 1 teaspoon baking soda
- ½ teaspoon salt
- 12 tablespoons (1½ sticks) cold, sweet butter
- 2 cups raisins, preferably gold
- 1 egg
- ½ cup honey
- 1 cup buttermilk

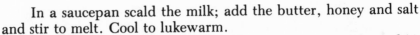

FOLARES (Portuguese Easter Loaves)

Use this same dough to make plain round loaves any time of year.

¾ cup milk

6 tablespoons sweet butter (¾ stick)

½ cup honey

1 teaspoon salt

2 tablespoons dry yeast

½ cup warm water

½ teaspoon sugar or honey

3 eggs

5½–6 cups unbleached white flour, approximately

10 hardboiled dyed eggs

In a saucepan scald the milk; add the butter, honey and salt and stir to melt. Cool to lukewarm.

In a large mixing bowl combine the yeast, warm water and ½ teaspoon sugar or honey. When it is bubbly, add the cooled milk mixture and eggs. Beat thoroughly. Add 3 cups of the flour and beat at least 200 strokes by hand or 2 minutes with an electric mixer. Gradually add more flour until the dough clings together and leaves the sides of the bowl. Turn out onto a floured board and knead until smooth and elastic, adding a little more flour as necessary. Try to keep a soft dough.

Put the dough in a buttered bowl, turn to coat all sides. Cover with a towel and let rise until doubled in bulk. Punch the dough down, turn out onto a lightly floured board, knead a few times to press out air bubbles, and cut into 10 equal pieces. Cover and let rest about 10 minutes. Take one piece of dough, leaving the rest covered, and cut off a quarter of it. Take the larger part and flatten it with your palm into a large round biscuit shape. Place it on a buttered baking sheet. Repeat with the remaining nine pieces, cutting off and reserving a quarter of each piece. Be sure there is plenty of space between your "biscuits" to allow for expansion (it will take several baking sheets; if you don't have enough, refrigerate the rest of the dough for later use). Brush the tops with melted butter and cover with a light towel. Let rest in a warm place for about 30 minutes.

Meanwhile take the smaller pieces of dough you have put aside and cut each one in half. Roll each half (20 in all) into a thin rope 6 to 8 inches long, or long enough to cross the biscuit with room to spare. Uncover the large biscuits and with your thumb or a spoon punch an indentation in the center of each one, deep enough to cradle an egg. Place a hardboiled egg into each concave nest, pressing it down gently. Take two of the long strips you have made and crisscross them over the egg at right angles, tucking each end underneath the biscuit-shaped piece of dough to hold the egg securely. If the strips aren't long enough, roll them some more to lengthen them. Brush the top of the dough with melted butter, cover with a light cloth and let rise until not quite double in bulk. Meanwhile preheat the oven to 350°F. Bake the folares about 25 minutes. Serve warm or cool on a rack.

Makes 10 small breads.

April

CREAM CHEESE SESAME BISCUITS

These are very tender.

2 tablespoons sesame seeds

1½ cups unbleached white flour

1½ teaspoons baking powder

½ teaspoon baking soda

¼ teaspoon salt

2 tablespoons cold vegetable shortening

2 tablespoons cold butter

1 beaten egg

⅓ cup buttermilk or sour milk

1 3-oz. package of cream cheese

Toast sesame seeds in a 350°F. oven about 20 minutes or until lightly brown.

Preheat oven to 425°F. Sift together flour, baking powder, soda and salt into a bowl. Work in butter and shortening with a pastry blender or two knives until the mixture resembles coarse meal. Toss in sesame seeds. Beat the egg. Add buttermilk and beat again. Dribble into the flour mixture while stirring with a fork. Turn dough out onto floured board and gather together with your hands. Knead gently about one-half minute, until it holds together. If necessary, use a pastry scraper to pull dough together. At this point dough may be wrapped well and refrigerated for up to 48 hours. Using a floured rolling pin, roll dough out very thin. Be sure there is enough flour on the board to keep the bottom from sticking. Cut with a round cutter dipped in flour. Place half of biscuits on ungreased baking sheet. Spread cream cheese over rounds on sheet. Top with other half of rounds, floured side up. Press gently.

Bake 10 to 12 minutes or until lightly browned. Serve hot.

This makes about 15 medium biscuits.

Note: Biscuits don't have to be baked immediately. Cover lightly and set them in a cool place for an hour or two. If you like, refrigerate overnight and bake for breakfast.

BROWN RICE BREAD

Coarse and chewy, with an earthy allure, it recycles some of the pots of leftover rice which seem always to be cluttering up the refrigerator.

In a saucepan scald the milk. Add the molasses, butter and salt, stir to melt and let cool to lukewarm.

In a large mixing bowl dissolve the yeast in the warm water with the ½ teaspoon sugar or honey. When frothy, add the cooled milk mixture, egg, and two cups of the flour. Beat two minutes with an electric mixer or at least 200 strokes by hand. Mix in the brown rice and currants. Gradually add more flour until the dough clings together and leaves the sides of the bowl.

Turn it out onto a floured board and knead until smooth and elastic, adding more flour as necessary. This dough will be *very* sticky, so be patient.

Put the dough in a buttered bowl, turn to coat all sides. Cover with a towel and let rise until doubled in bulk.

Punch the dough down, turn it out onto a lightly floured board, knead a few times to press out air bubbles and let rest, covered, for 10 minutes. Cut the dough into two pieces. Shape into oblongs and place in two 9-inch greased loaf pans. Cover and let rise until almost doubled.

Preheat the oven to 375°F. Bake about 35 to 40 minutes or until the bottoms sound hollow when tapped.

Remove from pans and cool on a rack.

Makes two large loaves.

1 cup milk

⅓ cup unsulphured molasses

2 tablespoons sweet butter or light oil

2 teaspoons salt or 1 teaspoon if rice was salted in cooking

1 tablespoon plus 1 teaspoon dry yeast

¼ cup warm water

½ teaspoon sugar or honey

1 egg

5 cups unbleached white flour, approximately. Use part whole wheat flour if you like.

2 cups cooked brown rice

⅓ cup dried currants

Kulich (Russian Easter) bread.

KULICH
(Russian Easter Bread)

This impressive bread is exultantly rich, with a cake-like texture. In Russia it is sliced in rounds and served with pashka, an even richer confection of pot cheese, butter, egg yolks, cream, sugar, nuts and candied fruits. For most of us a simple spread of sweet butter will suffice.

Scald the cream. Stir in honey, butter and salt. Cool to luke-warm. In a large mixing bowl combine yeast, warm water and ½ teaspoon honey or sugar. When yeast mixture is bubbly add the cooled cream mixture, vanilla and brandy. Beat to mix. Add egg yolks one at a time, beating well after each. Add 2 cups of flour and beat 2 minutes with an electric mixer or 200 strokes by hand.

In a separate bowl beat the egg whites with cream of tartar until they hold stiff peaks but are still glossy. Gently fold them into the batter. They don't have to be completely mixed in. Cover bowl and set in a warm place for an hour or so until the mixture has swollen and is frothy. Stir the sponge down and add enough flour to make a dough that holds together.

Turn dough out onto a floured board. Knead until smooth and elastic, adding as little flour as necessary for a'soft, tender dough. Place the dough in a buttered bowl, turn to coat all sides, cover with a towel and let rise until double in bulk.

Punch the dough down, turn out onto a lightly floured board, knead a few times to press out air bubbles, cover and let rest about 10 minutes.

Butter a tall round casserole or similar container, such as a 3-lb. coffee can. Form the dough into a round ball to fit container. It should fill container about ½ full. Brush the top with melted butter, cover and let rise, until almost doubled in size. Meanwhile, preheat oven to 350°F. Bake about 45 minutes. Remove and brush with *Glaze*: 1 whole egg beaten with 2 tablespoons cream or milk. Return to oven and bake another 15 minutes.

It's hazardous to take this bread out of the pan to test for doneness. Try inserting a cake tester into the center. It should come out easily and clean.

Let the Kulich sit in its pan for a few minutes before attempting to remove it. Then turn the pan on its side and carefully slide the bread out. Turn upright to cool on a rack. If the bread is not quite as crusty on the sides as you like just slide it back into the pan and bake for a few minutes longer. *For an extra fancy kulich . . .* add any or all of the following to the batter:

¼ teaspoon saffron threads soaked in one tablespoon of brandy or rum. Add with the cream.

⅓–½ cup each of slivered almonds, raisins and candied fruit. Add after stirring down sponge.

1½ tablespoons dry yeast
¼ cup warm water
½ teaspoon sugar or honey
1 cup cream
⅔ cup honey
6 tablespoons sweet butter (¾ stick)
1 teaspoon salt
1½ tablespoons dry yeast
¼ cup warm water
½ teaspoon sugar or honey
1 teaspoon vanilla
2 tablespoons brandy or an extra teaspoon vanilla
5 eggs, separated and at room temperature
1/8 teaspoon cream of tarter
6–7 cups unbleached white flour
1 egg plus 2 tablespoons cream or milk for glaze

SOURDOUGH BAGELS

The ones you make may not be as pretty as the ones you buy in the best bagel bakery you know, but they are more available if that bakery is 200 miles away. Also, the texture of these is somewhat less dense, but for a bagel addict the shape, aroma, flavor and scattering of poppy seeds are all irresistible.

1 cup sourdough starter

1½ cups warm water

2 cups unbleached white flour

½ tablespoon yeast

1 teaspoon honey

1 egg

3 tablespoons light oil

4 cups unbleached white flour, approximately

1 egg

Poppy seeds

In a large crockery, glass or plastic bowl mix together the starter, water and 2 cups flour. Cover tightly with a plastic wrap and let sit overnight or as long as 36 hours.

Add the yeast, honey, 1 egg and oil. Mix well. Begin adding flour, stirring until the dough becomes too stiff to stir. Turn out onto a floured surface and knead until smooth and elastic, adding a little more flour as necessary. Place the dough in a buttered bowl; turn to coat all sides. Cover with a towel and let rise until doubled in bulk. Punch the dough down, turn out onto a lightly floured surface, knead and cut with a knife into 14 to 16 equal pieces.

Shape each little piece into a rough ball. Cover and let rest 10 minutes. Roll each ball into a rope about 10 inches long. Dust the board with a bit of flour if dough is sticking. Take each little rope and form it into a circle. Pinch the ends together firmly from both top and bottom. Don't expect the final product to be completely symmetrical and don't worry that your pinching will mutilate the dough—better that than to have the circle come unglued during cooking.

Leave the circles with space between on the board where you shaped them. Cover with a towel; let rise until they are almost double in size.

Boil a great quantity of water in a very large pot (one you cook spaghetti in or one you use for canning). On an area near the stove spread out a double thickness of paper or cloth towels, enough to hold all the bagels with room to spare.

Preheat oven to 375°F. Dip a large egg-turner in flour, slide it deftly under the bagel and transfer it to a tray. Dip turner in flour each time you pick up a bagel. Be gentle lest you inadvertently depress one. When water is boiling fiercely, slide the bagels into the pot one at a time. Even a very large pot will only hold 3 or 4 at once. As soon as each bagel rises to the top, which is almost immediately, gently turn it over. Use two long-handled wooden spoons or a slotted metal spoon. After the bagels are turned cook 1 to 2 minutes more. Lift each one with a slotted spoon, drain over the pot and place on the towels.

When all the bagels have been cooked and drained, place on a greased baking sheet with room between. This will take at least two baking sheets, possibly three, and you will need to bake them in two batches. Slide you hand under the towel and tip it so the bagel falls in your other hand. If you use a spatula, pieces of paper towel may stick to the bagel.

Glaze: Beat the egg with 2 tablespoons cold water and brush over entire surface of bagels. Sprinkle liberally with poppy seeds or coarse salt or onion flakes. Bake about 20 minutes. The tops should be golden. Cool on racks.

These can be eaten any way, but they are never better than with a generous smear of cream cheese topped with some smoked salmon or whitefish, a little onion, a slice of tomato .

COLONIAL JOHNNYCAKES

The Rhode Island Johnnycake (nee Journeycake) one of the oldest, simplest and most venerable of American breads, is the heart of a continuing controversy. Spirited exchanges rage over the true historic method of making the johnnycake. Even the grease for the griddle is a matter for serious discussion. One list in descending order of desirability goes: rendered goose fat, duck fat, chicken fat, beef suet, vegetable oil and bacon fat (a last resort). All of these portentous questions have been taken under the wing of a worthy group called The Society for the Propagation of the Jonnycake Tradition in Rhode Island. Note their spelling of "jonnycake." Inquiries may be addressed to them at 70 Barnes Street, Providence, Rhode Island 02906. The recipe which follows is a slightly embellished version of the original but primitive enough to qualify.

Preheat a griddle or large heavy frying pan.

Pour the boiling water over the cornmeal and stir vigorously. Add the butter or lard and salt and mix until the butter is melted. Add enough more hot water to make a batter that will drop easily off a spoon and spread on the griddle to make a thin cake.

Grease the griddle—which should be moderately hot—lightly.

Pour on the batter with a serving spoon or large tablespoon. Fry like pancakes until golden brown on both sides. You may have to do a little experimenting with consistency of the batter and heat of the griddle. They should be thin and quite crisp.

1 cup boiling water
1 cup stone-ground cornmeal
2 tablespoons butter or lard
¼ teaspoon salt
½-¾ cup hot water, approximately

MAPLE BUTTERMILK MUFFINS

Light and crunchy.

1¾ cups unbleached white flour

1½ teaspoons baking powder

1 teaspoon baking soda

½ teaspoon salt

½ teaspoon cinnamon

2 eggs

⅓ cup buttermilk or sour milk

¼ cup melted sweet butter or light oil

½ cup maple syrup

¾ cup chopped pecans or walnuts

Preheat the oven to 400°F.

Sift together the flour, baking powder, soda, salt and cinnamon. In another bowl beat the eggs until light in color and slightly thickened. Add the buttermilk, melted butter and maple syrup and beat to mix. Stir in the nuts. Add the flour mixture. Blend with a rubber spatula or wooden spoon, stopping before flour is absorbed. Batter will be rough and lumpy.

Spoon batter into buttered muffin tins, filling each about ⅔ full. Bake 15 to 20 minutes.

This makes 12 to 14 medium muffins.

Martha Punderson makes muffins and the whole family likes them, including Rebecca the cow.

POSY'S HEALTHY CHALLAH

This is the classic Jewish braided egg bread, whose beauty is more than skin deep. It is light and rich, without being noticeably sweet. This version includes wheat germ, which deepens the golden glow and increases nutrition.

In a large mixing bowl combine the yeast with the ¾ cup warm water and teaspoon honey or sugar. Let it sit until bubbling. Add the 1 cup water, salt, butter and honey. Mix well. Add eggs one at a time, beating well after each. Add 4 cups flour. Beat 2 minutes with an electric beater or 200 strokes by hand. Add the wheat germ. Add enough remaining flour to make a dough that pulls away from the sides of the bowl and holds together.

Turn out onto a floured board and knead until smooth and elastic, adding a little more flour if dough remains sticky. Be sparing. Place dough in a large buttered bowl. Turn to coat all sides. Cover with a towel and let rise until doubled in bulk. Punch the dough down, turn out, knead briefly to press out air bubbles. Divide into 3 or 4 equal pieces. Cover and let rest 10 minutes.

Divide one ball of dough into three equal parts. Form each part into a rope about 18 inches long by rolling it against the board with your hands. Braid the three ropes. Pinch the ends together. Place in a 9-inch greased loaf pan.

Repeat with the other balls of dough. If you don't have enough loaf pans, braids may be baked on greased cookie sheets.

Brush tops of loaves with melted butter. Cover, let rise until doubled in bulk.

Preheat oven to 375°F.

Glaze: Blend the egg and butter. Brush it on tops of loaves. Sprinkle with poppy seeds if desired. Bake braids about 30 minutes, longer for larger braids. Don't let them cook too long which is easy to do because the bottom tends to stay soft and doesn't produce a hollow thump until almost too late.

If you prefer, make 3 large braids, or, if you can fathom it, the classic Hebrew 8 braid.

Makes 4 medium loaves, 3 large braids, 2 giant ones, or one gargantuan one.

2½ tablespoons dry yeast
¾ cup warm water
1 teaspoon honey or sugar
1 cup warm water
1 tablespoon salt
½ cup sweet butter, softened, or light oil
⅓ cup honey
7 large eggs
9 cups unbleached white flour, approximately
¾–1 cup raw wheat germ
1 egg and 1 tablespoon butter for glaze

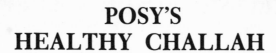

THREE SEED QUICK BREAD

This interesting bread is chewy, not especially sweet and makes crunchy toast.

¼ cup sunflower kernels

¼ cup sesame seeds

2 eggs

⅓ cup honey

1 cup buttermilk or fruit juice

1¾ cups unbleached white flour

2 teaspoons baking powder

1 teaspoon soda

½ teaspoon salt

¼ cup raw wheat germ

1 tablespoon caraway seeds

½ cup golden raisins

Toast sunflower kernels and sesame seeds on a baking sheet in a slow oven about 15 minutes. Remove seeds and preheat oven to 350°F.

In mixing bowl beat eggs until light in color. Add honey and buttermilk or juice. Beat again.

Sift together the flour, baking powder, soda and salt. Add wheat germ, caraway seeds, raisins and toasted seeds. Toss with two forks to distribute evenly.

Blend dry and wet ingredients, stirring lightly until just mixed. Pour batter into greased, medium-sized loaf pan. Bake 40 to 45 minutes or until the top feels springy when pressed with your finger. Cool loaf in its pan 10 minutes. Remove and finish cooling on a wire rack.

Makes one loaf.

RICOTTA PANCAKES

These tender pancakes are delicately scented with nutmeg.

3 eggs

1 cup ricotta cheese

3 tablespoons honey

5 tablespoons melted sweet butter

½ cup unbleached white flour

½ teaspoon baking powder

½ teaspoon salt

⅛ teaspoon nutmeg

In a blender combine eggs and cheese. Blend until light and fluffy. Add honey and butter. Blend again.

Sift together flour, baking powder, salt and nutmeg. Add to cheese mixture and blend together.

Preheat griddle or large heavy skillet. Grease lightly. Pour batter on, about 2 tablespoons at a time, to make small pancakes. Cook over medium heat until a few bubbles appear on the surface. Turn and brown the other side. The inside should still be moist. Serve at once or keep the done ones warm in a low oven while you finish.

Sprinkle tops with a bit more nutmeg, if desired. Serve with fruit, jam or maple syrup and perhaps a dollop of sour cream.

This makes about 30 small pancakes.

Note:

If you don't have a blender use an electric mixer. Beat eggs first until light in color and slightly thickened; add cheese and continue as directed.

YANKEE GRITS BREAD

Asked to describe this bread, its originators, Sam and Sheila Ogden, came up with a thoughtful "good." A bit more pondering produced "crusty," "chewy," "a little sweet." All of which are true. It's made with bacon, eggs, milk and grits and from a Southern point of view that's a complete breakfast in every slice.

In a large bowl dissolve yeast in the ½ cup warm water with the teaspoon sugar or honey. When bubbling add second ½ cup water, honey, egg, bacon grease, salt and 2 cups of the flour. Beat 2 minutes with an electric beater or 200 strokes by hand. Add grits and dry milk. Gradually add about 4 cups flour or enough to make a dough that is too stiff to beat and pulls away from the sides of the bowl.

Turn dough out onto floured board and knead until smooth and elastic. Fortify yourself for a long haul. This dough takes a lot of kneading and will try to thwart you by remaining persistently sticky. Add a little more flour as necessary to handle. When dough is good and elastic, it will still be a bit tacky. Put it in a buttered bowl, turn to coat all sides, cover with a towel and let rise until doubled in bulk.

Punch dough down and if time permits let it rise a second time in the bowl. Punch it down again and turn out onto a floured board. Knead a few times to press out air bubbles. Cut in half, cover and let rest 10 minutes. Shape each half into a loaf and put in 9-inch buttered loaf pans. Brush the tops with melted butter. Cover and let rise until not quite double in size.

Preheat the oven to 375°F. Bake about 40 minutes or until the bottoms of the loaves sound hollow when thumped.

Remove from pans and cool on a rack. Crusty, chewy, a little sweet, and good.

Makes two generous loaves.

½ cup warm water
1½ tablespoons dry yeast
1 teaspoon sugar or honey
½ cup water
⅓ cup honey
1 egg
3 tablespoons bacon grease or light oil
2 teaspoons salt
6 to 7 cups unbleached white flour
1½ cups warm grits cooked without salt
¾ cup dry milk

SWEDISH CARAWAY BREAD

A pleasantly mild and versatile bread.

Excellent

4.5	1½ tablespoons dry yeast 3
6	2 cups warm water 4
1.5	½ teaspoon honey or sugar 1
3	1 cup unbleached white flour 2
1.5c	½ cup honey 1
6T	2 tablespoons sweet butter, melted or light oil 4
6TP	2 teaspoons salt 4
3T	1 tablespoon caraway seeds 2
9C	3 cups unbleached white flour, approximately 6
6C	2 cups rye flour, preferably stone-ground 4

In a large mixing bowl combine the yeast with 1 cup of the water and ½ teaspoon sugar or honey. Stir. Add 1 cup white flour; mix well. Cover the bowl with a cloth or plastic wrap and let it sit for anywhere from ½ hour to overnight. (Refrigerate if leaving it for more than a few hours.)

When ready to proceed, add the second cup warm water, honey, butter, salt, caraway seeds and 2 cups of the white flour. Beat 2 minutes with an electric mixer or at least 200 strokes by hand. Add rye flour and a little more white flour if necessary to make a dough that pulls away from the sides of the bowl.

Turn dough out onto a floured board; knead until smooth and elastic, adding a little more white flour if the dough remains too sticky.

Put the dough into a buttered bowl; turn to coat all sides. Cover with a towel and let it rise until double in bulk.

Punch the dough down, turn it out onto the board, knead briefly to press out air bubbles, cut in half, cover and let rest about 10 minutes.

Grease two medium-sized loaf pans. Shape dough into loaves. Place in pans. Brush tops with melted butter, cover and let rise until almost doubled in size.

Bake in preheated 350°F. oven about 40 minutes or until bottoms of loaves sound hollow when tapped. Cool on rack.

Makes 2 loaves.

May

CORTLANDT'S POTATO ROLLS

These are very light and have a luscious texture.

2 tablespoons dry yeast

1 cup warm potato water (water in which potatoes have been cooked)

½ teaspoon sugar or honey

¾ cup butter and vegetable shortening, mixed in whatever proportions you like

½-¾ cup honey, according to preference

2 eggs

2 teaspoons salt

1 cup warm mashed potatoes

7 cups unbleached white flour

In a large bowl dissolve the yeast in ½ cup of the warm potato water with the ½ teaspoon sugar or honey. Let it sit until bubbly. Melt butter and shortening. Cool. Add remaining ½ cup potato water, butter and shortening, honey, eggs, salt and mashed potatoes to the yeast and beat all together. Add 2½ cups flour and beat with an electric mixer 2 minutes or at least 200 strokes by hand. Gradually add 3½ to 4½ cups more flour, or enough to make a dough that clings together and leaves the sides of the bowl. Turn the dough out onto a floured board and knead until smooth and elastic, sprinkling with a little more flour if it remains too sticky. Exercise restraint and expect it to be clingy. Put the dough into a buttered bowl, turn over to coat all sides. Cover with a cloth and let rise until doubled in bulk.

Punch the dough down, turn it out onto a lightly floured board and knead a few times to press out air bubbles. Cut the dough into 32 pieces. The easiest way is to cut the dough in half, cut each half in half, etc. Cover pieces of dough and let rest 10 to 15 minutes. Shape into whatever kind of rolls you desire. Cover and let rise until not quite double. Preheat oven to 450°F. Bake 10 to 15 minutes, depending upon size, or until golden and done. Serve hot. If serving later, cool on a rack.

If you plan to freeze rolls, remove from the oven when just beginning to turn color. Cool, freeze in a plastic bag, and finish cooking when ready to use. This method prevents them from drying out when reheated. These rolls may be shaped, brushed with melted butter, covered with a damp cloth and put in the refrigerator to rise slowly until the next day. Then you can have rolls hot from the oven with all the work having been done in advance.

CORA'S REAL SOUTHERN CORN BREAD

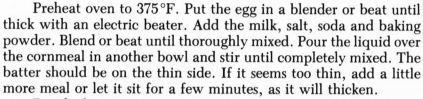

As everyone knows, or will know, Southern corn bread uses no sweetening of any sort, is made with white cornmeal and uses no flour. Southerners feel any other version is corrupt. The author of this recipe adds, "Don't even bother to make this unless you can get fresh, white stone-ground meal."

Crisp, not sweet, and bitey with whole grain meal, this rather austere corn bread may require an acquired taste. A taste that for some has become a passion.

Preheat oven to 375°F. Put the egg in a blender or beat until thick with an electric beater. Add the milk, salt, soda and baking powder. Blend or beat until thoroughly mixed. Pour the liquid over the cornmeal in another bowl and stir until completely mixed. The batter should be on the thin side. If it seems too thin, add a little more meal or let it sit for a few minutes, as it will thicken.

Put the bacon grease or oil in a heavy, 7-inch cast-iron skillet. Heat on top of the stove until the grease is spitting hot. Carefully tilt the pan to and fro so the sides will get greased, too.

Pour in the batter and let it cook on top of the stove for a couple of minutes to make a crisp, brown bottom crust. Then bake in the oven until the center is firm, about 20 minutes.

This makes six good but not greedy pieces. The recipe can easily be doubled, but the batter should fill the pan so use a 9- to 10-inch skillet. If you've been asked to bring the loaves for someone else's fishes, a pan of corn bread goes a long way.

1 egg

1 cup buttermilk or sour milk or thin yogurt, or sweet milk mixed with one teaspoon vinegar

1 teaspoon salt

1 teaspoon baking soda

2 teaspoons baking powder

1 cup white stone-ground cornmeal

3-4 tablespoons bacon grease or other cooking oil

Antique tin for corn breads.

ORANGE RICOTTA BREAD

Delicately perfumed with orange and anise.

1½ tablespoons dry yeast

½ cup warm water

½ teaspoon sugar or honey

½ cup orange juice

⅓ cup honey

2 eggs

2 tablespoons light oil

2 teaspoons salt

1 teaspoon anise seed

4 teaspoons grated orange peel

1 cup ricotta cheese or cottage cheese

6 cups unbleached white flour

In a large mixing bowl dissolve the yeast in the warm water with the half teaspoon sugar or honey. Let it sit until bubbly. Add the orange juice, honey, eggs, oil, salt, anise, orange peel and ricotta. Beat well. Add 2 cups of the flour and beat 2 minutes with an electric mixer or at least 200 strokes by hand. Gradually add 3 to 4 cups more flour or as much as it takes to make a dough that pulls away from the sides of the bowl. Turn the dough out onto a floured board and knead until smooth and elastic, sprinkling on a little more flour if it remains too sticky.

Put the dough into a buttered bowl, turn to coat all sides, cover with a towel and let it rise until doubled in bulk.

Punch dough down, turn it out onto the board, knead a few times to press out air bubbles, cut in half, cover and let rest 10 minutes.

Grease two 9-inch loaf pans. Shape the dough to fit, place in pans. Brush tops with melted butter. Cover and let rise again until almost doubled in size.

Preheat the oven to 375°F. Bake 30 minutes, or until the bottoms sound hollow when tapped. Cool on a rack.

Makes two loaves.

CHOCOLATE QUICK BREAD

This loaf is very dark, rich and moist and, surprisingly, not very sweet. Serve for tea with butter, cream cheese or jam.

2 oz. unsweetened chocolate

⅓ cup sweet butter

2 eggs

⅓ cup honey

1 cup warm mashed potatoes (in a pinch, use instant)

¼ cup rum, brandy or orange juice

1 teaspoon vanilla

1 teaspoon grated orange peel

1½ cups unbleached white flour

2 teaspoons baking powder

½ teaspoon salt

Preheat oven to 350°F. Melt the chocolate and butter together. In a mixing bowl beat the eggs until light and thick. Beat in the honey, potatoes, chocolate and butter, rum, vanilla and orange peel.

Sift together the flour, baking powder and salt. Combine with liquid ingredients and fold together, until just mixed. Pour batter into a greased loaf pan and bake 50 to 55 minutes or until the top feels springy. Let it sit in its pan for 10 minutes before removing to cool on a rack.

For a sweeter chocolate bread, use 2 oz. semi-sweet chocolate and ½ cup honey. This version is nice for tea or dessert or as an accompaniment for fruit.

Makes one loaf.

SOURDOUGH ENGLISH MUFFINS

These have a more authentic texture and taste than plain yeasted ones, without being any more trouble. Chewy, with the characteristic uneven holes inside and a somewhat hard crust, they also proclaim a distinctive sourdough flavor.

½ cup sourdough starter
1 cup milk
3 cups unbleached white flour
1 teaspoon salt
1 teaspoon baking soda
1 teaspoon baking powder
1 tablespoon sugar
Cornmeal

In a large glass, plastic or crockery bowl mix together the starter, milk and 1½ cups of flour. Cover the bowl with plastic wrap and leave in a warm place overnight, or up to 24 hours. This is known as a sponge.

The next day sift together remaining 1½ cups flour, salt, soda, baking powder and sugar. Add this to the sponge, mix, and, if you have time, cover and let it rest 30 to 60 minutes.

Stir down the dough and turn out onto a floured surface. The dough will probably be loose, depending on the quality and activity level of your sourdough starter. With floured hands gently gather the dough together and knead it briefly until it begins to feel cohesive and somewhat resilient. You may have to keep sprinkling it with flour. The kneading should take only one or two minutes.

With your hands pat the dough out into a rough circle about ½-inch thick. Cut out rounds with a large cookie cutter, glass or tin can. Dip the cutter in flour each time. Place the rounds on an ungreased baking sheet liberally sprinkled with cornmeal. Dust the tops with more cornmeal. Cover and let rise in a warm place 45 minutes to an hour. The rising will not be dramatic—that happens on the griddle.

Heat a griddle or heavy cast-iron frying pan on top of the stove. (An electric frying pan also works well.) The heat should be low to medium low. You have to experiment to see what works best for you, but I find that low heat allows the muffins to cook all the way through without getting too brown on the outside. Sprinkle griddle with cornmeal. Do not grease. Thoroughly preheat. Place muffins on the griddle and bake until they have puffed up and browned somewhat on the bottom.

Turn and brown on the other side. They may turn only a delicate brown, which is fine. Baking takes between 15 and 25 minutes, depending on heat and size of muffins. An ideal state of doneness is reached when they are slightly hard on the top and bottom but moist inside, without being doughy. With your finger push gently on the top; if it is somewhat crusty but the muffin gives, that's a good sign. Or sacrifice one by splitting it open to check the inside. Don't cook too long or they'll get tough.

Eat while warm or cool on a rack, split later (with a fork) and toast.

Makes 8-11 muffins, depending on size.

MARMALADE QUICK BREAD

A moist, crunchy, piquat bread that is especially good for tea or dessert. Marmalades do vary in degree of sweetness which will affect, somewhat, the flavor of the bread.

1 egg

⅓ cup honey

½ cup melted sweet butter (1 stick)

½ cup orange juice

½ cup orange or other marmalade (the combination lemon, orange, and grapefruit is noteworthy)

2 tablespoons rum (or orange juice)

1 cup chopped walnuts or almonds

2 cups unbleached white flour. If marmalade is very runny, add ¼ cup more flour

2 teaspoons baking powder

½ teaspoon baking soda

½ teaspoon salt

Preheat oven to 350°F. In a large mixing bowl beat the egg until light in color. Beat in honey, melted butter, orange juice, marmalade and rum. Stir in the chopped nuts. Sift together the flour, baking powder, soda and salt. Combine with liquid mixture and stir until just mixed. Pour batter into a greased loaf pan and bake 50 minutes or until the top feels springy. Let the loaf sit in its pan 10-15 minutes before removing to cool on a rack.

Makes 1 loaf.

Antique bread board and knife.

IRENE'S ANADAMA WITH WHEAT GERM AND HONEY

This delightful, if unorthodox, version of a classic loaf makes delicious toast and keeps unusually well.

In a large mixing bowl dissolve the yeast in the half-cup warm water with the teaspoon sugar or honey. When bubbly, add the 1½ cups warm water, butter or oil, honey, salt, and 3 cups of the flour. Beat with an electric mixer 2 minutes or at least 200 strokes by hand. Mix in the cornmeal and wheat germ. Gradually add more flour, mixing until the dough clings together and leaves the sides of the bowl.

Turn the dough out onto a floured surface and knead until smooth and elastic, adding a little more flour as necessary if the dough remains too sticky to work with. Be patient and allow time for the gluten to develop; this dough continues to cling to your fingers because of the cornmeal and there is a danger of adding too much flour.

Put the dough into a buttered bowl, turn to coat all sides. Cover with a towel and let rise until double in bulk. Punch the dough down, turn out onto a lightly floured surface, knead a few times to press out air bubbles, cut in half, cover and let rest about 10 minutes. Shape dough into loaves and place in two 9-inch buttered loaf pans. Brush the tops with melted butter. Cover and let rise again until almost doubled in size.

Preheat the oven to 375°F. Bake 30 to 35 minutes or until the bottoms of the loaves sound hollow when thumped. Remove loaves from pans and cool on a rack.

Makes 2 large loaves.

½ cup warm water
2 tablespoons yeast
1 teaspoon sugar or honey
1½ cups warm water
⅓ cup melted sweet butter or oil
⅔ cup honey
2 teaspoons salt
6 cups unbleached white flour, approximately
1 cup cornmeal, preferably stone-ground
¼ cup wheat germ

VERMONT JOHNNYCAKE BREAD

A light sumptuous and slightly sweet corn bread which has nothing in common with Rhode Island Johnnycake except its name.

1¼ cups unbleached white flour

1½ teaspoons baking powder

½ teaspoon baking soda

½ teaspoon salt

½ cup stone-ground cornmeal (no other kind will give the proper crunch)

1 egg

1 cup buttermilk or sour milk

¼ cup maple syrup or honey

¼ cup melted sweet butter

Preheat the oven to 400°F. Sift together the flour, baking powder, soda and salt. Stir in the cornmeal and mix well with a fork. Beat the egg until light and slightly thickened. Add the buttermilk, maple syrup or honey and melted butter and beat again. Combine with the flour-cornmeal mixture and blend gently with a rubber spatula or wooden spoon. Pour batter into a buttered 8-inch square pan. Bake about 25 to 30 minutes or until the center is set. It will feel springy. Serve hot with butter, honey or jam, although it's rich enough to eat plain. And practically ambrosial to split, butter and toast later under the broiler.

BRAN BUTTERMILK BISCUITS

Pleasantly nutty and just faintly sweet.

1¾ cups unbleached white flour

1½ teaspoons baking powder

½ teaspoon baking soda

½ teaspoon salt

1 tablespoon sugar

½ cup bran flakes (not cereal)

3 tablespoons cold sweet butter

3 tablespoons cold vegetable shortening

1 egg

½ cup buttermilk or sour milk

Sift together the flour, baking powder, soda, salt and sugar. Mix in the bran flakes with a fork. Cut in the butter and shortening with a pastry blender or two knives until the mixture resembles coarse meal. Beat the egg and mix with the buttermilk. Dribble into the flour and toss with a fork to mix. Turn the dough out onto a floured board and knead lightly about a half-minute; using a pastry scraper helps. (At this point you can wrap the dough in wax paper and refrigerate up to 48 hours.)

With a floured rolling pin, roll the dough out on a lightly floured board ¼ to ⅓ inch thick. Cut with a cookie or biscuit cutter dipped in flour. Transfer to ungreased baking sheet. Cover with a light cloth and let sit 30 minutes or longer (even overnight in the refrigerator). Preheat the oven to 425°F. Just before baking, brush the tops with melted butter. Bake 10 minutes or until golden. The time will depend on the thickness of the biscuits. Remove and split one to test for doneness. Serve hot.

This makes about 16 medium biscuits.

FRENCH TOAST
(Pain Perdu)

The name comes from the French and literally means "lost" bread. This elegant Creole recipe is a far cry from the soggy slices one often encounters under this title and is a fine example of creative recycling.

Slice some stale homemade bread. White bread is traditional but not a must. Cut off the crusts and cut into rounds, diamonds or triangles, one or two per slice. Beat the eggs until they are very light in color and thick. Add the cream, honey, orange flower water or orange juice, brandy or rum, orange peel and salt. Beat together to mix well. In a large skillet heat 1½ inches cooking oil to 350°F.

Dip each piece of bread in the egg mixture, coating it thoroughly on both sides. Drop each piece in the hot fat, making sure not to crowd the pan. You will have to do it in several batches. Fry each piece until it is brown and crisp-looking on the underside, then turn with a spatula and repeat.

Drain the pieces on paper towels and continue frying until all the pieces are done. Arrange them on a platter and sprinkle generously with powdered sugar and perhaps a little grated nutmeg. Serve with maple syrup, jam, fresh berries, yogurt, or all of the above.

This amount of egg mixture is enough for 6 or 7 whole slices of bread, which will mean 12 to 14 smaller pieces. The recipe can easily be doubled and probably should be if you are making it for more than three people, unless they're all on diets.

2 eggs
¼ cup heavy cream (or light cream or half and half)
2 tablespoons honey
1 tablespoon orange flower water or 1 tablespoon orange juice
1 tablespoon brandy or rum
½ teaspoon grated orange peel
⅛ teaspoon salt

Furniture executive Leo Heer bakes French bread in full regalia.

SOURDOUGH FRENCH BREAD

You can approximate the distinctive taste and texture of San Francisco French bread (which is different from French French bread). The secret is not the recipe but the method, and some experimentation will reveal what works best for you. The sourness of the bread is determined by the length of time you leave the sponge. Since most people identify this bread with a decided tartness, you may wish to let the sponge work for at least 24 hours.

In a large glass, plastic or crockery bowl mix together the starter, warm water and 2 cups flour. Cover with plastic wrap and leave at room temperature overnight or as long as 48 hours. Add the yeast, honey, and salt. Beat, then add enough flour to make a dough that clings together and leaves the sides of the bowl. Turn out onto a floured surface and knead until smooth and elastic, adding a bit more flour if the dough remains too sticky. Place the dough in a buttered bowl. Turn to coat all sides. Cover with a towel and let rise until doubled in bulk. Punch the dough down, turn out onto a lightly floured surface and knead a few times to press out air bubbles. Cover, let rest about 10 minutes.

Now you must decide how many loaves you wish to make. This will depend on your preference and the kind of pans you have. This amount of dough will make two large loaves or as many as six slender baguettes the traditional shape and size for French bread. Baguettes will also provide the most authentic taste because of the ratio of crust to insides. But they are more difficult to form unless you have a special French bread pan with diminutive scoops for the dough. The easiest way is to divide the dough into four or five equal pieces. Shape each into a long sausage by rolling it with your palms against the board.

Carefully place loaves on greased baking sheets dusted with cornmeal. Leave some space between loaves as they spread more out than up as they rise. If you have French bread pans, form the appropriate number of loaves and place them in the greased spaces. Make three long diagonal slashes about ¼-inch deep across each loaf with a razor blade or sharp knife. Cover with a very light towel. Let rise until the loaves have almost doubled in size.

Preheat oven to 425°F. Have ready a kettle of boiling water. Place a large shallow pan on the bottom of the oven. Place baking sheet with risen loaves on middle rack of oven. Pour boiling water into pan. Close oven door immediately.

After 5 minutes brush loaves with cold water or use an atomizer or plant mister to spray loaves with cold water. After a second five minutes brush or spray loaves again with water and remove pan of boiling water from the oven. Reduce heat to 375°F and continue baking. Little loaves may take only 10 minutes more, large ones as much as 30 minutes.

Loaves should sound hollow when tapped on the bottom and be a beautiful crusty brown. Cool on racks. French bread really should be eaten the day it is baked. Cut on the diagonal with a good bread knife or tear apart with your fingers.

Loaves that won't be eaten that day can be frozen after cooling.

1 cup sourdough starter
1¼ cups warm water
2 cups unbleached white flour
½ tablespoon dry yeast
2 teaspoons honey
2 teaspoons salt
3 cups unbleached white flour, approximately

SWEDISH LIMPA BREAD

*Several elusive flavors are blended in this delicious rye bread.
Nice for toast too.*

¼ cup cracked wheat

2 tablespoons sweet butter
or light oil

¼ cup unsulphured
molasses plus
2 tablespoons honey

1 teaspoon caraway seeds

½ teaspoon fennel seeds

½ teaspoon cumin seeds

2 teaspoons salt

½ cup milk

1 cup water

1½ tablespoons dry yeast

½ cup warm water

½ teaspoon sugar or honey

1 cup whole wheat flour,
preferably stone-ground

2 cups unbleached white
flour

1 tablespoon grated
orange peel

2 cups rye flour,
preferably
stone-ground
Cornmeal

In a heat-proof bowl combine the cracked wheat, butter, molasses, honey, caraway, fennel and cumin seeds and salt. Combine the milk and 1 cup water in a saucepan and bring just to boiling. Pour over the cracked wheat mixture and stir to mix. Cool to lukewarm.

In a large mixing bowl combine the yeast with ½ cup warm water and ½ teaspoon sugar or honey. Stir to mix. Let it sit until bubbly. Add the flour—cracked wheat mixture to the yeast. Add the whole wheat, 1½ cups of the white flour and the orange peel. Beat with an electric mixer 2 minutes or at least 200 strokes by hand.

Cover the bowl and let it sit in a warm place about an hour. Check it once in a while to make sure the sponge isn't bubbling up and over the sides. Stir the sponge down and add the rye flour, mixing with a wooden spoon until the dough clings together and leaves the sides of the bowl. Turn the dough out onto a lightly floured board and knead, sprinkling on a little more white flour if it remains too sticky. When it becomes elastic, even if it is still somewhat clingy, you can stop. Put the dough in a buttered bowl and turn to coat all sides. Cover with towel and let rise until doubled in size. Punch the dough down, turn it out onto a board, knead a few times to press out air bubbles, cut it in half, cover with the towel and let it rest about 10 minutes.

Form each half into an oval-shaped loaf and place on a greased baking sheet that has been dusted with cornmeal. With a sharp knife make several short slashes crosswise on the tops. Cover and let rise again until almost doubled.

Preheat oven to 350°F. Bake about 40 to 50 minutes or until the bottoms sound hollow when tapped. Cool on a rack.

Makes two loaves.

June

Wedding bread from Crete (unbaked).

WEDDING BREAD FROM CRETE

A visually spectacular, fragrant and spicy bread. You will probably only undertake this for a special occasion, but that doesn't have to be a wedding.

In a sauce pan combine the milk and ½ cup water. Bring just to a boil, remove from heat, add butter, honey and ouzo. Stir to melt butter. Cool.

In a large mixing bowl combine the yeast, ½ cup warm water and ½ teaspoon sugar or honey. When bubbly, add the cooled milk mixture, eggs, spices, peels, anise seeds and salt. Beat well. Add 3 cups of the flour and beat at least 200 strokes by hand or 2 minutes with an electric mixer. Gradually add more flour until the dough clings together and leaves the sides of the bowl. Turn out onto a floured board and knead until smooth and elastic, adding a little more flour as necessary but keep the dough on the soft side. Put the dough in a buttered bowl, turn over to coat all sides. Cover with a towel and let rise until doubled in bulk. Punch the dough down, turn out onto a floured board, knead a few times to press out air bubbles. Cut off about ⅓ of the dough. Cover both pieces and let rest 10 minutes. Take the larger piece of dough and roll it with your hands into a long rope. (Do this on a large table.) The rope should be smooth, of uniform thickness, and long enough to make a circle that will fit on your largest baking sheet with room all around for expansion. Form the rope into a doughnut, seal ends and place on a buttered baking sheet. Cover with a towel.

Now take the smaller piece of dough and on a lightly floured board roll it out with a rolling pin like pie dough as thin as possible. Cut out decorative shapes to go all over the top and sides of your circle. Use either small cookie cutters or a sharp knife. You get more fanciful shapes if you do it freehand but for most of us the cookie cutters are probably a better bet. Dip the cutters or your knife into flour before cutting out each shape. Stars, trees, flowers, leaves, birds, animals, circles, crescents, crosses, diamonds, little people are all appropriate.

You may also want to make some tiny braids criss-cross the dough among your other shapes. Lift the cut-outs with a floured spatula to the edge of the board. Gather up the leftover dough to reroll and cut more designs. You will need more than you think because as the bread expands it stretches the decorations apart from each other. Remove the towel from your large circle and cover it closely with the cutouts, pressing them slightly to help them adhere. They may be stuck on at random or in some design. Braids look best if placed symmetrically. Brush the loaf all over with a mixture of egg white beaten slightly with a tablespoon of water. Cover with a light cloth and let rise about 45 minutes to an hour in a warm place. The loaf should be noticeably swollen but not doubled. Preheat the oven to 350°F. Bake the loaf about 50 minutes, or until brown and crusty all over and a toothpick stuck deeply in the side comes out clean. (Forget about trying to lift it to tap the bottom.) If the decorations seem to be browning too quickly, cover the bread loosely with foil.

With pancake turners carefully lift the bread to a large rack to cool (or slide it off if your sheet has no sides). Serve with sweet butter. Just assume a cavalier attitude when people cut right into your masterpiece.

½ cup milk

½ cup water

¼ lb. sweet butter (1 stick)

½ cup honey

2 tablespoons ouzo, rum or vodka (or orange juice)

2 tablespoons dry yeast

½ cup warm water

½ teaspoon sugar or honey

3 eggs

¼ teaspoon mahaleb (optional)

½ teaspoon cinnamon

½ teaspoon grated orange peel

½ teaspoon grated lemon peel

¾–1 teaspoon anise seeds, depending on how definite a flavor you like (if using ouzo, reduce anise to ½ teaspoon)

1 teaspoon salt

7–7½ cups unbleached white flour

Egg white for glaze

BRIDE'S BREAD

Not for brides only, yet, scented with oranges and spiked with almonds, it smells just like a wedding.

- 2 eggs
- ½ cup honey
- ⅓ cup orange juice
- ⅓ cup light oil or melted sweet butter
- 2 tablespoons Cointreau or other orange liquor or rum
- ¼ teaspoon almond extract
- 1 tablespoon freshly grated orange peel
- 1 cup blanched sliced almonds
- 1 cup unbleached white flour
- 1 cup rye flour, preferably stone-ground
- 2 teaspoons baking powder
- ½ teaspoon baking soda
- ½ teaspoon salt
- ½ teaspoon ground cardamon
- ¼ teaspoon ground allspice

Preheat the oven to 325°F. In a large bowl beat the eggs until light and slightly thickened. Add the honey and beat well. Beat in the orange juice, oil or butter, Cointreau, almond extract and orange peel. Stir in the almonds.

Sift together the white and rye flours, baking powder, soda, salt, cardamon and allspice. Gently fold together the flour and liquid mixtures until just mixed. Pour batter into a buttered loaf pan or round oval casserole. Bake 40 minutes, or until the top feels springy when pressed and the bread is brown around the edges. Don't overcook.

Cool in the pan about 10 minutes before removing to cool on a rack. Feel free to sniff frequently.

Makes one loaf.

Wedding bread from Crete at wedding of Wendy & Sandy Noyes.

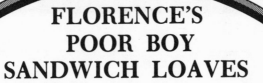

FLORENCE'S POOR BOY SANDWICH LOAVES

If you look into your cupboard and find only a chunk of cheese or a can of tuna, no matter. Whatever is there can be transformed into a lusty lunch if you call it a poor boy sandwich, and you can if you have a bag of these aromatic loaves in your freezer. Wrapped loosely in foil, they can be thawed and warmed in the oven in about 15 minutes, which will give you time to search the corners and crannies. The concept of a poor boy is to be a catch-all for any number of odd ingredients, the more outrageous in nature and quality, the better. This bread is flavored with rye and caraway, which is a good foil for practically anything.

In a large bowl dissolve the yeast in the ½ cup warm water with the teaspoon sugar or honey. When bubbly, add the water, molasses, butter or oil, salt, seeds and 3 cups white flour. Beat with an electric mixer 2 minutes or at least 200 strokes by hand. Add the rye flour, and enough more white to make a dough that clings together and leaves the sides of the bowl.

Turn the dough out onto a floured board and knead until smooth and elastic, sprinkling with more white flour to make dough workable. Put the dough in a buttered bowl; turn over to coat all sides. Cover with a cloth and let rise until doubled in bulk.

Punch the dough down, turn out onto a lightly floured board, knead a few times to press out air bubbles and cut into 8 equal pieces. Cover and let rest 10 to 15 minutes. Shape each piece into a ball. Roll out with a lightly floured rolling pin into an oval 6 to 7 inches long. Starting with a long side, roll the dough up tightly like a cigar. Press the long seam gently into the dough to seal it, pinch the ends together to seal them and place the roll, seam side down, on a buttered baking sheet. Brush the tops with melted butter, cover and let rise until not quite double in size. Preheat oven to 375°F. Bake 15 minutes, then brush rolls with an egg white beaten with 1 tablespoon water. Continue baking about five minutes longer. Don't overbake; they should be soft on the inside. Cool on a rack.

This makes 8 loaves.

1½ tablespoons dry yeast

½ cup warm water

1 teaspoon sugar or honey

1½ cups water

⅓ cup unsulphured molasses

4 tablespoons melted sweet butter or light oil

1 tablespoon salt

2 teaspoons caraway seeds (or 1 teaspoon each caraway and fennel)

4 cups unbleached white flour

2 cups rye flour, preferably stone-ground

Egg white for glaze

Cinnamon rolls.

CINNAMON ROLLS

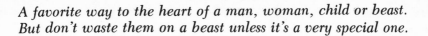

A favorite way to the heart of a man, woman, child or beast.
But don't waste them on a beast unless it's a very special one.

Make the dough as described in Farmhouse Bread. After it has risen once in the bowl, punch it down, turn out onto a floured board, knead a few times and cut in half. Cover and let rest 10 minutes. With a floured rolling pin, roll each half into a rectangle about ¼-inch thick. The dough may resist you at first, but keep at it and it will eventually roll out.

Spread each half with the soft butter. You can be liberal or abstemious, in keeping with your scruples or diet. Mix together the cinnamon and sugar and sprinkle evenly over the dough. Top with finely chopped nuts if you desire. Roll up each rectangle tightly like a jelly roll, starting with a long side.

With a sharp knife, slice the roll at 1-inch intervals to make little pinwheels. Place these cut side up, on a greased baking sheet and brush with melted butter. Cover with a light cloth and let rise until almost double in size.

Preheat the oven to 400°F. Sprinkle the tops of the rolls with a little more cinnamon sugar, if you like, and bake about 15 to 20 minutes, or until golden and done.

Pull one apart to test. If you plan to freeze some for later use, take them out a couple of minutes early. Cool on a rack.

These rolls adapt very well to the vagaries of your schedule. If you would like to have them for breakfast make them up the night before. Place on baking sheets, brush liberally with melted butter, cover with damp cloths, refrigerate to rise overnight. In the morning preheat the oven. If rolls haven't risen quite enough, put them on top of the stove to warm as oven heats. If really rushed, place them directly in cold oven and turn on to 400°F. They will rise some as the oven heats. In this case judging doneness is a little more difficult—you can always try one.

If you wish to freeze for later, place a baking sheet of rolls in the freezer, before their final rise. Freeze. Package in plastic bags. When ready to use, put rolls on greased baking sheet to thaw and rise at room temperature. Brush again with melted butter before baking, and sprinkle with a little more cinnamon sugar, if desired. Cooked rolls can be frozen.

This recipe makes 24 to 30 rolls.

Use the recipe for
Farmhouse Bread
on page 157.
In addition to
those ingredients,
you will need:

¼–½ **cup very soft sweet butter**

2 **tablespoons cinnamon**

¼ **cup sugar, brown sugar or raw sugar**

Finely chopped nuts (optional)

pretty good
1-87
kids liked
not too goo-ey

CRISP CORN BREAD

½ cup unbleached white flour

½ teaspoon baking powder

1 teaspoon baking soda

½ teaspoon salt

1 cup cornmeal, preferably stone-ground

2 eggs

1 tablespoon honey

1½ cups buttermilk or sour milk

2 tablespoons melted butter

*Pretty good
could be sweeter
11-22-86*

Sift together the flour, baking powder, soda and salt. Mix in the cornmeal with a fork. Preheat the oven to 425°F.

In another bowl beat the eggs until they are light in color and slightly thick. Add the honey, buttermilk and melted butter and beat to mix. Blend with the flour mixture. The batter will be thin.

Grease a jelly roll pan (about 15 × 11-inches) with lard, bacon grease or meat drippings. Put it in the oven until the pan and grease are very hot. Pour the batter onto the pan, spreading into the corners, and bake until golden and crisp, about 15 to 20 minutes. Cut in squares and serve hot.

About 15 pieces.

Flour bag attached to chute to be filled.

MOROCCAN SESAME ANISE BREAD

The interesting flavor of these fat loaves would spark an early summer picnic or buffet supper.

In a saucepan scald the milk. Add the butter, honey, salt and seeds. Cool.

In a large mixing bowl dissolve the yeast in the warm water with the ½ teaspoon sugar or honey. When bubbly, add the cooled milk mixture, 2 cups white flour and ½ cup whole wheat flour. Beat with an electric mixer 2 minutes or at least 200 strokes by hand.

Gradually add 2 more cups whole wheat flour until the dough clings together and leaves the sides of the bowl.

Turn the dough out onto a floured surface and knead until smooth and elastic, gradually kneading in any remaining whole wheat flour if the dough remains too sticky to work with. If you have used all the whole wheat, use a little more white flour.

Put the dough in a buttered bowl and turn to coat all sides. Cover with a towel and let rise until it has doubled in bulk.

Punch the dough down, turn out onto a lightly floured surface, knead a few times to press out air bubbles, cut in half, cover and let rest 10 minutes.

Grease a large baking sheet and dust with cornmeal. Shape the pieces of dough into two smooth plump balls and carefully place on the baking sheet, leaving room between them. With a sharp knife cut a small cross in the top of each loaf. Brush with butter; cover and let rise until almost doubled.

Preheat the oven to 375°F. Bake about 30 minutes or until the bottoms sound hollow when tapped. If you wish, about 10 minutes before you expect loaves to be done brush them with a glaze of one whole egg beaten with 2 tablespoons water. Sprinkle sesame seeds over the tops.

Cool the loaves on a rack.

Makes two round loaves.

¾ cup milk

2 tablespoons sweet butter or light oil

2 tablespoons honey

2 teaspoons salt

2 teaspoons anise seed

1 tablespoon sesame seed

1 cup warm water

1 tablespoon yeast

½ teaspoon sugar or honey

2½ cups whole wheat flour, preferably stone-ground

2 cups unbleached white flour

egg for glaze
sesame seeds

Sharing a grape and a doughnut.

*Billy can't resist a doughnut at
his mother's roadside stand.*

QUICK WHOLE WHEAT BUTTERMILK DOUGHNUTS

•

These easy doughnuts are crunchy and somewhat sweet, with a barely perceptible flavor of molasses. Just plain good. And still good the next day if any are left.

In a large bowl beat the eggs until they are light in color and thickened. Add the honey, molasses, buttermilk and melted butter and beat to mix.

Sift together the white flour, salt, baking powder and soda. Add 2 cups of the whole wheat flour and mix well with a fork. Combine flour and egg mixtures and stir gently. Add more of the whole wheat flour if the mixture is too wet to hold together.

Turn the dough out onto a floured board and gather it together with your hands, then knead lightly until it holds together. A pastry scraper is helpful in pulling the sticky dough together in the beginning. Add more whole wheat flour as necessary, but the dough should be as soft as possible and still be manageable. Wrap the dough in plastic and chill for 30 minutes to an hour, or more.

On a lightly floured board roll the dough out about ½-inch thick with a floured rolling pin. Cut out with a doughnut cutter or two biscuit cutters (one large for the doughnuts, one quite small for the holes). Let the doughnuts and their holes rest 10 to 15 minutes, uncovered.

In a deep pot heat 3 or 4 inches of oil to 360°–375°F. Use a frying thermometer and leave it in the pot to help you keep a steady temperature.

Slide the doughnuts, one at a time, from a spatula into the hot oil. Cook only a few at once (don't crowd the pot). Fry until golden brown on the bottom; turn and repeat. This should take only 2 to 2½ minutes. Remove with a slotted spoon and drain on paper towels or, following an old convention, on a brown paper bag. Before you proceed, break open one to check for proper doneness. The tendency is to cook them too long which makes them dry.

When you have fried all the doughnuts, fry the holes. These will take even less time. Or fry the holes first, especially if you have children panting at your knee. While still warm roll the doughnuts and their holes in cinnamon sugar, if desired.

This makes about 18 medium sized doughnuts.

2 eggs
¼ cup honey
¼ cup unsulphured molasses
1 cup buttermilk
2 tablespoons melted sweet butter
¾ cup unbleached white flour
½ teaspoon salt
1 teaspoon baking powder
1 teaspoon baking soda
3 cups whole wheat flour, preferably stone-ground

RHUBARB BREAD

"Rhubarb is certainly hard to purée," remarked my mother-in-law, Virginia Glendinning Johnson Taylor. "Its very life is in its strings." No need to purée it here; just chop it up to make a fresh, piquant, juicy loaf.

1 egg

1 cup honey

½ cup melted butter

½ cup orange juice or pineapple juice

1½ cups finely chopped raw rhubarb

¾ cup chopped nuts

2½ cups unbleached white flour

2 teaspoons baking powder

½ teaspoon baking soda

½ teaspoon salt

¼ teaspoon powdered ginger

Preheat oven to 350°F. In a mixing bowl beat the egg with the honey, melted butter and orange juice. Stir in the rhubarb and nuts. Sift together the flour, baking powder, soda, salt and ginger. Combine dry and wet ingredients, stirring just to mix. Pour the batter into 2 small to medium sized, greased loaf pans. Bake 35 to 40 minutes or until the tops feel springy to the touch. Cool bread in pans 10 minutes before removing to cool on a rack.

Makes two loaves.

CHAPPATIS

These flat Indian breads are kneaded but unleavened, easy to put together, and a pleasant accompaniment to most any meal. Torn apart, they are also useful as food holders or shovelers, which is how they are used in India. They can be made from a number of different grains.

Mix together the white flour, salt, and the 2 cups of the other flour or flours you are using. Add the melted butter and toss lightly with a fork. Continue tossing as you add enough warm water to make a dough that is quite soft but not wet. This will average around 1½ cups. You don't want a stiff dough, even though it is easier to work with. If you get it a little too wet sprinkle in a little more flour. The dough will firm up somewhat as it is kneaded. Turn the dough out onto a floured board and knead thoroughly, about 10 minutes by hand (or 5 minutes if you have a mixer with a dough hook).

Dust the ball of dough with flour and wrap in wax paper or a damp towel and chill for an hour or longer. Cut the dough in half, cut each half in half, then cut each quarter into three pieces, ending up with 12 equal lumps of dough.

Form each lump into a ball, press to flatten slightly and roll out on a lightly floured board with a floured rolling pin into a large irregular circle that is uniformly paper thin (or as close to that as you can get). The thorough kneading makes the dough elastic enough to be rolled to this thinness.

Preheat a griddle or large heavy skillet over medium heat. Wipe the griddle surface with a greased paper towel.

Place the first chappati on the griddle and bake until slightly browned on the bottom, turn and repeat on the other side. Maintain the heat at medium to medium-high. It will take 3 to 4 minutes for the chappati to be cooked through, light brown on both sides, but **not crisp**. Ideally, it should be still pliable, but if you overdo it, don't fret, you'll just have a cracker. While the first one is cooking (don't forget to turn it!) roll out the next one. Continue until all are cooked keeping the done ones warm in a low oven. Brush with butter and serve while warm. You may need to wipe the griddle with a greased paper towel between each one.

Having made chappatis with all five of the flours mentioned, I still can't decide on a favorite, unless perhaps it is the rolled oats. . . . but then the graham flour is sweetly nutty . . . . and the barley is interesting. Oh well, chappatis are welcome in any dress.

- 2 cups unbleached white flour
- 1 teaspoon salt
- 2 cups stone-ground whole wheat flour, or graham flour, rolled oats, barley flour, or rice flour
- 3 tablespoons melted butter
- 1–1¾ cups warm water

MIDNIGHT SUN CREPES

This adaptation of a Scandinavian recipe was named for its versatility. The batter, which yields very tender and only faintly sweet crepes, can be made up in advance and used in any number of ways for breakfast, lunch, dinner, dessert or a midnight snack.

3 eggs
1½ cups milk
3 tablespoons melted sweet butter
1 tablespoon honey
¾ cup unbleached white flour
¼ teaspoon salt
⅛–¼ teaspoon nutmeg

In a large bowl beat the eggs until they are very light and frothy. Beat in the milk, melted butter and honey. Sift together the flour, salt and nutmeg. Add to liquid ingredients. Beat well to blend. The batter will be thin. Refrigerate until ready to use but allow to warm a bit and beat again before cooking.

Preheat a crepe pan over moderate heat. A 5- to 6-inch heavy skillet with sloping sides may be used. Lightly grease pan for the first crepe. Do not grease again. Pour in about 3 tablespoons of batter and tilt the pan so the batter will flow and evenly cover the bottom. Less batter, though slightly more difficult to turn, will produce a thinner and more delicate crepe. When the crepe begins to turn brown around the edges, gently lift the edge with a fork to check the bottom. When it is lightly browned, slip an egg turner underneath (using the fork to help lift the edge) and turn. Allow to get brown and slightly crisp on the other side. Keep warm in a low oven on a large platter. Do not stack them.

When ready to serve, put about 2 tablespoons of filling on crepe, then fold, place seam side down and add a topping if appropriate.

Here are a few ideas for serving:

Breakfast: Fill with plain yogurt, sprinkle tops liberally with cinnamon sugar.
Fill with yogurt sweetened with a little honey and top with fresh fruit or berries.
Fill with sour cream sweetened with maple syrup. Top with slivered almonds.
Fill with lingonberries and sprinkle tops with sugar.
Fill with fruit jam and crown with a dollop of yogurt or sour cream.

Lunch or Supper: Fill with cottage cheese, mixed with herbs, celery seeds or dill seeds.
Fill with salmon, crab, chicken or turkey.
Try sautéed seasoned mushrooms, asparagus or creamed spinach.
Dress them with a hollandaise or lightly curried cream sauce.

Dessert: Fill with fresh sliced strawberries, sprinkle with sugar and top with sour cream or vanilla ice cream. Roll unfilled crepes, sprinkle the tops with sugar and lavishly spoon fresh berries or sliced peaches around them.
Fill with a lemon sauce or curd, sprinkle with powdered sugar and fresh raspberries.

Midnight snack: Any of the above or, if your imagination is burning bright, think up something new.

This makes 16 to 18 crepes.

July

CUMIN BREAD

With a fine, slightly chewy texture, this aromatic loaf presents orange and cumin in an unexpected harmony.

1 cup milk

½ cup honey

6 tablespoons sweet butter
(¾ stick) or light oil

2 teaspoons salt

1 tablespoon cumin seed

1½ tablespoons dry yeast

¼ cup warm water

½ teaspoon sugar or honey

1 cup orange juice

3 cups unbleached white
flour

3 cups stone-ground whole
wheat flour

In a saucepan scald the milk, add the honey, butter, salt and cumin seed, stir to melt the butter and let it sit until lukewarm.

In a large mixing bowl combine the yeast and warm water with the half teaspoon sugar or honey. Let it sit until bubbly.

Add the lukewarm milk mixture to the yeast, along with the orange juice and 3 cups white flour. Beat 2 minutes with an electric mixer or at least 200 strokes by hand.

Gradually add the whole wheat flour, as much as it takes to make a dough that clings together and pulls away from the sides of the bowl.

Turn the dough out onto a board dusted with flour and knead until smooth and elastic, sprinkling with a little more whole wheat flour if it remains too sticky. Be patient and be sparing with the flour.

Put the dough into a buttered bowl, turn it over or brush the top with melted butter, cover with a kitchen towel and let it rise until double in size.

Punch the dough down, turn it out onto the lightly floured board, cut in half, cover with the towel and let it rest for about 10 minutes.

Grease 2 medium to large loaf pans. Shape the dough to fit the pans, put it in, brush the tops with melted butter, cover with the towel and let rise again until almost double.

Preheat oven to 375°F. Bake 30 to 35 minutes or until the bottoms sound hollow when tapped. Cool on a rack.

Makes 2 loaves.

LACY CORN CAKES

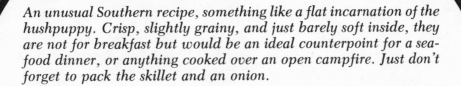

An unusual Southern recipe, something like a flat incarnation of the hushpuppy. Crisp, slightly grainy, and just barely soft inside, they are not for breakfast but would be an ideal counterpoint for a sea-food dinner, or anything cooked over an open campfire. Just don't forget to pack the skillet and an onion.

Bring the water to a boil and pour it over the cornmeal in a heat-proof bowl, stirring vigorously with a whisk or fork to get a smooth mixture. Immediately add the grease or butter and minced onion and stir until evenly mixed, then add flour, salt and pepper and stir again. In another bowl beat the egg until very frothy and add it to the meal mixture when the latter has cooled just enough so that it won't cook the egg. Mix well. The batter will be quite thin. Preheat a griddle or skillet to moderately hot and grease lightly with oil or drippings.

Drop the batter on about 2 tablespoons at a time to make small pancakes. The first few will be experimental. If the heat is right and the batter thin enough, the cakes will spread out flat and will form tiny holes all the way through as they cook (thus the allusion to lace). Very likely the batter will not be thin enough and you may want to stir in 2 tablespoons to ¼ cup more *cold* water. Also, the cornmeal will absorb moisture as it sits and the batter may have to be thinned again before you are finished.

Fry the cakes until brown on the bottom, then turn. Inspect the first batch for holes and thinness, then, unless a ravenous mouth is waiting, discard, as they will be greasy. It probably won't be necessary to grease the skillet or griddle again. Stir the batter in the bowl well each time before dipping into it with your spoon to keep the ingredients evenly distributed. The cakes should come off the griddle deep golden brown on both sides, dotted with tiny holes, crisp but not stiff on the outside and with just a micrometer of melting softness within. Drain them on paper towels and eat with your fingers while hot.

You have to try these to see how simple they are, and then you'll be glad as you munch on a fresh fish and a savory corn cake, or two, or ten.

Makes about 24 thin cakes.

1½ cups water

¾ cup cornmeal, preferably stone-ground

2 tablespoons bacon grease, meat drippings, or melted butter

2 tablespoons very finely minced onion

2½ tablespoons unbleached white flour

½ teaspoon salt
   Several good shakes of white pepper

1 egg
   Cold water as needed

Mary Partridge works beaten biscuits through a meat grinder.

CORA'S BEATEN BISCUITS

Beaten biscuits are an old Southern tradition, once ubiquitous, now rare. The strenuous exertions involved have fallen into disfavor, along with the disappearance of "kitchen help" who could be left to carry it out while the "lady" of the house arranged flowers.

Beaten biscuits weren't found only on the tables of gentry, however; to the ordinary housewife as well they were all in a day's work. Old recipes call for pounding the dough with a rolling pin or mallet until blisters formed on the surface, which might take 30 minutes or longer. Since there are few such strong arms extant, an alternative is to push the dough through a meat grinder or food chopper. It still takes time but much less heft. The result of all your trouble is a multitude of tiny golden biscuits with a unique crumbly texture. Whether they are worth it you will have to decide, but anyone who knows about such things will be impressed that you actually did it.

Start with 5 cups of the flour. Sift with the sugar, salt and baking powder. Cut in the lard or shortening with a pastry blender or two knives. Add the milk and mix well. You should have a stiff dough. Add more flour as necessary to produce such.

Run handfuls of the dough through the medium blade of a food chopper. The entire quantity of dough should be run through 6 or 8 times. It's a mess, but intriguing to watch. At first the dough comes out in little worm-like squiggles. Gradually, the squiggles become longer and hold together until you have handfuls of thick spaghetti. At this point you have worked it enough.

Preheat the oven to 350°F. Roll out the dough on a lightly floured board about ¼ inch thick. Cut out with a small (about 1-inch) cookie cutter or, according to one source, a syrup pitcher top.

Put on ungreased baking sheets and prick each biscuit with a fork. Bake about 20 minutes or until light brown on top. Eat hot or cold. They keep well for at least a couple of days.

Asked for the quantity of this recipe, Cora says it makes "a helluvalot."

Probably around six dozen diminutive biscuits.

6 cups unbleached white flour, approximately

1 teaspoon sugar

1 teaspoon salt

1 teaspoon baking powder

1 cup lard

1 cup milk

BATTER BROWN BREAD

Very good good flavor & texture

2 tablespoons dry yeast
½ cup water
1 teaspoon sugar or honey
2 teaspoons salt
⅓ cup molasses
1½ cups warm water
2 eggs
2 cups unbleached white flour
4 cups whole wheat flour, approximately, preferably stone-ground
¼ cup cornmeal, preferably stone-ground

This is a compact loaf with a finer crumb than most batter breads. It is crunchy and has an excellent flavor. A fine accompaniment to a summer ham supper or vegetarian feast fresh from the garden.

In a large bowl dissolve the yeast in the ½ cup water with the teaspoon sugar or honey. When it is bubbling add the salt, molasses, 1½ cups water and eggs and beat well to mix. Add 2 cups white flour and 1 cup whole wheat and beat very thoroughly for 5 to 10 minutes. Add the cornmeal and, gradually, about 3 more cups whole wheat flour, stirring vigorously until the dough clings together and leaves the sides of the bowl.

Cover and let the dough rise in its bowl until it has doubled in size.

Punch the dough down and, if you have time, let it rise again in the bowl. Stir it down with a wooden spoon and divide it equally between two buttered, medium (about 8 × 5-inch) loaf pans. Cover the pans and let the dough rise until it reaches or almost reaches the tops of the pans.

Preheat the oven to 375°F. Bake about 25 minutes or until the loaves sound hollow when thumped on the bottom. Cool on rack.

Makes two small-to-medium loaves.

WHEAT GERM HAMBURGER BUNS

The nobility of the all-American hamburger is revealed anew in homemade hamburger rolls. These are fortified with wheat germ. They can also be made into hot dog rolls. Make a batch, freeze, remove as needed and warm in the oven. The only hazard is that you may be permanently turned off the kind of ersatz hamburgers in make-believe muffins served by commercial establishments. There really is no place like home.

In a saucepan scald the milk. Add the butter, honey and salt and let cool to lukewarm.

In a large bowl dissolve the yeast in the ½ cup warm water with the ½ teaspoon sugar or honey. When it is bubbling, add the cooled milk mixture, eggs and 3 cups of the flour. Beat with an electric mixer 2 minutes or at least 200 strokes by hand. Stir in the wheat germ. Gradually add 3 more cups flour, or enough to make a dough that clings together and leaves the sides of the bowl. Turn the dough out onto a floured board and knead until smooth and elastic, sprinkling with a little more flour if it remains sticky. Put the dough in a buttered bowl, turn to coat all sides or brush the top with melted butter. Cover with a cloth and let rise until doubled in bulk. Punch the dough down, turn out onto a floured board and knead a few times to press out air bubbles.

Divide into 12 equal pieces (cut in half, each half in half and each quarter into 3 parts). Cover with a cloth and let rest for 10 to 15 minutes. Form each piece into a ball by rolling between the palms or by pressing into a thick pancake and tucking all the edges underneath and pinching them together (the latter method gives a smoother top surface). Put the balls on a greased baking sheet or sheets, prettiest side up, leaving plenty of room between them, and press each one lightly with your palm to flatten it just a bit. Brush the top with melted butter.

For hot dog rolls, roll out each ball with a floured pin into a flat oval, then roll up tightly like a cigar, pinch the ends together, press the seam so it will not come apart and place seam-side-down on baking sheets.

Cover the rolls lightly and let rise until not quite double in size. Meanwhile preheat the oven to 400°F. Bake about 15 to 20 minutes.

Don't let them overcook.

Cool on racks. Makes 12 rolls.

1½ cups milk

4 tablespoons sweet butter or light oil

1–2 tablespoons honey, according to taste (some people are morally opposed to a hint of sweetness in their hamburger buns)

2 teaspoons salt

½ cup warm water

1 tablespoon plus 1 teaspoon dry yeast

½ teaspoon sugar or honey

2 eggs

6 cups unbleached white flour, approximately

¾ cup wheat germ

SWEET ZUCCHINI BREAD

In this fragrant loaf the chameleon quality of zucchini is enveloped by other sensations of spiciness, softness and crunchiness. This will take care of at least one of your excess squashes.

1 egg

½ cup honey

⅓ cup melted sweet butter or light oil or a mixture.

1 teaspoon vanilla

1½ cups grated or shredded zucchini, skin and all

½ cup gold raisins

½ cup chopped nuts

1½ cups unbleached white flour

2 teaspoons baking powder

½ teaspoon salt

1½ teaspoons cinnamon

Preheat the oven to 350°F.

In a mixing bowl beat the egg until it is light and thick. Add the honey, butter or oil and vanilla and beat well to blend. Stir in the zucchini, then the raisins and nuts, and mix. Sift together the flour, baking powder, salt and cinnamon. Add the flour mixture to the liquids and fold in with a rubber spatula, mixing lightly until the flour is just absorbed.

Pour the batter into a buttered, medium to large loaf pan. Bake about 45 to 50 minutes or until the top feels springy to the touch. Let the bread sit in its pan for about 10 minutes before removing to cool on a rack.

Makes one loaf.

CREAM SHORTCAKES

These fluffy and slightly sweet biscuits are the traditional base for fruit shortcakes (strawberry, peach, or whatever) but also make delicious dinner biscuits. They are fluffy when hot, dense and flaky when cool.

2 cups unbleached white flour

1 tablespoon baking powder

½ teaspoon salt

1 tablespoon sugar

3 tablespoons cold sweet butter

3 tablespoons cold vegetable shortening

1 cup heavy cream

Preheat the oven to 425°F.

Sift together the flour, baking powder, salt and sugar. Cut in the butter and shortening with a pastry blender or two knives until the mixture is evenly but coarsely textured, about the size of tiny peas. Sprinkle in the cream and toss with a fork. Turn the dough out onto a floured board and gather it together with your hands. Knead gently a few times just until it clings together. With a floured rolling pin, roll out the dough ¾ inch to 1 inch thick for shortcakes (thinner for regular biscuits). Cut with a large cookie cutter (3- to 4-inch), glass or tin can, dipped in flour.

For regular biscuits cut with a smaller cutter. Carefully remove the rounds to an ungreased baking sheet by sliding a floured egg turner under them. Gather up the scraps of dough on the board, re-roll and re-cut. Bake about 20 minutes for shortcakes, 12–15 for biscuits.

Break one open to test. Cool on a rack. This makes 10–12 shortcakes.

CRACKLING CORN BREAD

•

To some this will be a bizarre combination, but it has a solid place in traditional Southern country cooking. For me it will always recall the panoramic picnic lunch that followed my grandmother's funeral in northwest Georgia. I was impressed by the gravity of the occasion, the numbers of kinfolk, known and unknown, the abundance of food and specifically the crackling corn bread. Though I had spent part of many summers in those mountains and had in fact been raised on fried chickens (alive that very morning in my grandfather's back yard), beans cooked with ham hocks for epic periods of time, and Georgia peaches, sublime in any form, never before had I encountered crackling corn bread. This late acquaintance was a puzzle because it seemed that of all the dear and familiar foods at the funeral banquet, crackling corn bread was in some way the most basic.

Cut the pork fat or salt pork into small dice and fry them over medium heat until they are quite crisp and brown, but not burned. Drain and cool on paper towels, reserving the grease. You should end up with about ½ cup of cracklings.

Preheat the oven to 425°F.

Sift together the flour, baking powder, soda and salt (if using). Mix in the cornmeal with a fork.

In another bowl beat the eggs until quite frothy. Beat in the honey and buttermilk. Stir in the cracklings. Add the cornmeal mixture and blend gently but thoroughly with a rubber spatula or wooden spoon.

Grease a 9- to 10-inch heavy skillet with about 2 tablespoons of the leftover grease from the cracklings. Put in the oven until it is quite hot. Pour in the batter and bake about 30 minutes, or until the center feels gently firm. Cut in wedges to serve. And don't wait for a funeral.

1⅓ cups fresh pork fat or salt pork, enough to make ½ cup of cracklings

¾ cup unbleached white flour

1½ teaspoons baking powder

1 teaspoon baking soda

½ teaspoon salt, if using fresh pork fat (omit if using salt pork)

1 cup cornmeal, preferably stone-ground

2 eggs

2 teaspoons honey (optional—mellowing but not authentically Southern)

1 cup buttermilk or sour milk

Making doughnuts in Maine (machine automatically cooks them correctly).

YOGURT DOUGHNUTS

The lovely confections are best eaten right away.
Which should pose no problem.

In a large bowl beat the eggs until they are light in color and somewhat thickened. Beat in honey, yogurt and melted butter.

Sift together the flour, salt, nutmeg, soda and baking powder. Combine this with the yogurt mixture, blend gently and turn out onto a lightly floured board. Pat the dough together with your hands and knead it gently a few times until it holds together. A pastry scraper is helpful in folding the dough over on itself. If the dough seems quite sticky add a little more flour.

Wrap the dough in plastic or wax paper and chill for 30 minutes to an hour (or longer).

Roll the dough out on a lightly floured board with a floured rolling pin to about ½-inch thickness. Cut with a doughnut cutter or two biscuit cutters (one large, one small). Dip the cutters in flour each time. Let the doughnuts and their holes rest on the board for 10 to 15 minutes, uncovered.

Heat deep fat or oil in a deeper pot to 375°F. If you have one, use a candy thermometer and leave it in the pot so you can constantly check the temperature.

Place the doughnuts on a spatula and slide them, one at a time, into the hot fat. Cook only a few at once; don't crowd the pot. Fry until golden brown on both sides, about 3 minutes in all. Remove with a slotted spoon and drain on paper towels or, following tradition, on a brown paper bag. Break open one of the first ones to test for proper doneness. Repeat frying with remaining doughnuts and their holes.

These doughnuts are not sweet. You may dust them with powdered sugar, glaze them with an icing of powdered sugar and a little water, or roll in cinnamon sugar.

Makes about 18 medium-sized doughnuts (also 18 holes).

2 eggs
¼ cup honey
1 cup plain yogurt
2 tablespoons melted sweet butter
3 cups unbleached white flour
½ teaspoon salt
¼ teaspoon nutmeg
1 teaspoon baking soda
1 teaspoon baking powder

SOUR MILK QUICK BREAD

There are numerous variations on this theme. You can use all whole wheat flour, all white, part oatmeal or corn meal, you can sweeten it with brown sugar, molasses or honey, add whatever fruits and nuts you have on hand, or make it plain. A good way to clean out the cupboard. Dark, sweet, crunchy, and good to eat, too.

1 cup sour milk*
½ cup maple syrup
⅔ cup gold raisins
½-1 cup chopped nuts
1 cup unbleached white flour
1 cup rye flour, preferably stone-ground
½ teaspoon salt
1½ teaspoons baking powder
1 teaspoon baking soda
½ teaspoon allspice
¼ teaspoon nutmeg
1 teaspoon cinnamon

Preheat oven to 350°F. In a mixing bowl combine the sour milk and maple syrup. Stir in the raisins and nuts.

Sift together the flours, salt, baking powder, soda, all spices. Add this to the batter. Stir together until just blended.

Pour into a large buttered loaf pan or casserole and bake 45-50 minutes. This may get done before it tests done; push down on the top gently with your finger; if it is no longer squishy but still resilient, it's probably done.

Let the bread sit in its pan about 10 minutes before removing to cool on a rack. Slice thinly and serve with whipped cream cheese.

Makes one large loaf.

To sour milk, stir 1 tablespoon lemon juice or vinegar into 1 cup milk and let stand in a warm place 5 to 10 minutes. Using old milk that has gone bad is not recommended. Buttermilk is fine.

Sacks of grain stacked, waiting to be ground in the Falls Mills Grist Mill in Tennessee.

SALLY'S LAMB ROAST BREAD

No need to wait for a lamb roast to bake this toothsome variation of the classic Anadama.

In a saucepan scald the milk. Stir in the butter or oil, molasses and salt. Let cool to lukewarm.

In a large mixing bowl dissolve the yeast in the warm water with the ½ teaspoon sugar or honey. When bubbly, add the cooled milk mixture and 3 cups of the white flour. Beat thoroughly with an electric mixer 2 minutes or at least 200 strokes by hand. Slowly stir in the cornmeal, add the sunflower seeds and rye flour, mix, then gradually add enough more white flour to make a dough that clings together and leaves the sides of the bowl. Turn the dough out onto a floured board and knead until smooth and elastic, adding a little more white flour as necessary. Expect this dough to remain somewhat clingy. Put the dough into a buttered bowl, turn to coat or brush the top with melted butter. Cover with a damp towel and let rise until doubled in bulk.

Punch the dough down, turn it out onto a lightly floured board, knead a few times to press out air bubbles, cut into 2 or 3 pieces, cover with towel and let rest about 10 minutes. Butter 3 medium loaf pans or 2 large ones. Shape the dough into oblongs and place in pans. Brush the tops with melted butter. Or you can make free-form loaves to put on a buttered cookie sheet which is dusted with cornmeal.

Cover the loaves with a damp towel and let rise again until almost doubled.

Preheat the oven to 375°F. Bake 30 minutes for medium loaves, 40 minutes for large, or until the bottom of the loaves sound hollow when tapped (time will vary according to size). If you like, brush the loaves with an egg glaze (whole egg beaten with a tablespoon milk or water) about 10 minutes before you expect them to be done.

Remove from pans to cool on a rack.

Makes two or three loaves.

1¾ cups milk
¼ cup sweet butter or light oil
½ cup molasses
1 tablespoon salt
1½ tablespoons dry yeast
½ cup warm water
½ teaspoon sugar or honey
4½-5 cups unbleached white flour
⅔ cup cornmeal, preferably stone-ground
¼-⅓ cup sunflower kernels
1 cup rye flour, preferably stone-ground

SWANS ISLAND BLUEBERRY DROP BISCUITS

Wonderfully fresh for a summer meal, especially if you have spent an hour gathering your own wild blueberries. Actually, it takes much less than an hour to get a cup of berries but you must take into account the number which will evaporate into your mouth. These biscuits are not sweet. Serve with butter and honey.

2 cups unbleached white flour

1 tablespoon baking powder

½ teaspoon salt

3 tablespoons cold sweet butter

1 cup cold milk

1 cup fresh blueberries, washed and drained on a towel, then tossed with 2 tablespoons sugar

Preheat the oven to 375°F.

Sift together the flour, baking powder and salt. Cut in the butter with a pastry blender or two knives until the mixture is coarsely textured. Pour in the milk and mix gently with a fork. Before completely mixed, add the berries and continue mixing with a large spoon—gingerly so as not to bruise the berries.

Drop the batter by spoonfuls onto a buttered baking sheet. If you wish, sprinkle a little more sugar over the biscuits before baking. Bake for 20 to 25 minutes or until lightly browned. The time will depend on their size. Break one open to test. Serve immediately.

This will make 12 large biscuits.

August

CORN BREAD WITH FRESH CORN AND CREAM

Here is one good thing to do with ears of corn that don't get eaten, if such a fate should ever befall you.

¾ cup unbleached white flour

1 tablespoon baking powder

½ teaspoon salt

1 cup cornmeal, preferably stone-ground

2 eggs

1 tablespoon honey

1 cup heavy cream

1 cup cooked corn kernels, cut off the cob

Preheat the oven to 425°F.

Sift together the flour, baking powder and salt. Mix in the cornmeal with a fork.

In another bowl beat the eggs until light-colored and slightly thickened. Add the honey and beat, then the cream and combine thoroughly. Stir in the corn. Lastly, add the flour mixture and mix well.

Heat a 9- or 10-inch skillet on top of the stove and grease it with about 2 tablespoons bacon grease, cooking oil, lard or clarified butter. Let it get good and hot. Pour in the batter and bake for 30 to 35 minutes, or until the middle is set.

Cut in wedges to serve. Makes about 10 generous servings.

Corn bread for a summer picnic.

CORN BREAD IN A BAG

For an emergency or a whim.

This is an adaptation of a very old recipe. If you find yourself in a campground or on the frozen tundra without an oven for baking, you can still concoct something on this order, using whatever ingredients you have. You may or may not like the result but you'll probably enjoy the process.

Pour the boiling water over the cornmeal and stir vigorously. Mix flour, baking powder, salt and soda together well with a fork. Beat eggs until light and thick. Beat in molasses and ½ cup milk. Stir in raisins, flour mixture and cornmeal. If the batter seems quite stiff, add a little more milk. It is preferable to have a loose batter, but it must be thick enough not to leak through the bag.

Pour the batter into a tightly woven cloth bag (such as the kind that dried beans sometimes come in), or a linen dish towel, or several layers of cheesecloth, or anything else that's clean and available. Tie the ends so that the batter is completely enclosed, making sure you have left room for the dough to expand as it cools (the bag should be almost twice as big as the dough).

If you have a colander or steamer which fits inside a large pot, use this. Put some water in the pot and bring it to a boil. It should not reach high enough to come through the colander and touch the bag. If you don't have a colander, tie a string to the bag and suspend it over the side of the pot, again not allowing it to touch the boiling water.

Cover the pot with foil, if available, and then its cover, so that it is as tightly closed as possible. You will need to check it now and again and replenish the water, which tends to boil away. Let the bag steam 2½ to 3 hours. You can press the bag to tell when the consistency is no longer mushy. The dough will also stiffen a bit as it cools.

Remove the bag and let it cool a few minutes. Unwrap bread or dig it out of the bag. Break off pieces with a fork and serve warm with butter.

1½ cups cornmeal, preferably stone-ground
1 cup boiling water
1 cup unbleached white flour
1 teaspoon baking powder
½ teaspoon salt
¼ teaspoon baking soda
2 eggs
¼ cup molasses
½–⅔ cup milk
½ cup gold raisins

SOURDOUGH BISCUITS

1 cup unbleached white flour

¼ teaspoon baking soda

2 teaspoons baking powder

¼ teaspoon salt

⅓ cup sweet butter (5⅓ tablespoons) or vegetable shortening

1 cup sourdough starter

Sift together the flour, soda, baking powder and salt.

Cut in the butter or shortening with a pastry blender or two knives until coarsely textured and reasonably well distributed.

Add the sourdough starter and mix gently.

Turn the dough out onto a lightly floured board and knead about 10 times.

Pat the dough out into a rough rectangle and then roll it out with a rolling pin until it's about ½-inch thick.

Cut out biscuits of whatever size you wish and place on a greased baking sheet. Take the scraps of dough, form them into a ball and roll out again to make more biscuits.

Cover and let the biscuits rise about 30 minutes. Preheat the oven to 425°F.

Brush the tops of the biscuits with melted butter just before putting them in the oven.

Bake 7-10 minutes.

Makes about 12 biscuits.

BREAD CRUMB PANCAKES

This is an old recipe and a good way to use stale bread. It contains no sweetener so serve with fruit, jam or maple syrup.

1½ cups breadcrumbs made by grating stale homemade bread

1½ cups milk

½ cup unbleached white flour

½ teaspoon salt

1 teaspoon baking powder

2 eggs

2 tablespoons melted sweet butter

Soak the breadcrumbs in the milk briefly.

Sift together the flour, salt and baking powder. Beat the eggs until they are light in color and thickened. Add the crumb mixture and the melted butter, beating well to blend, then the flour, mixing again.

Preheat a griddle or large heavy skillet and grease lightly. Drop the batter on the griddle, which should be medium hot, about 2 tablespoons at a time. The pancakes should be small. When they are brown and crisp on one side, turn and brown on the other. You may have to brush on just a bit more oil with a pastry brush between batches.

As with all pancakes, they are best served right off the griddle, but you can also keep them warm on a platter in a low oven while you finish frying the rest.

Makes about 24 small pancakes.

FRESH HERB BREAD

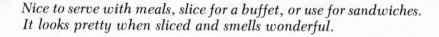

Nice to serve with meals, slice for a buffet, or use for sandwiches.
It looks pretty when sliced and smells wonderful.

In a large saucepan bring the milk just to a boil. Remove from heat; add butter, mashed potatoes and honey. Stir with a wire whisk to blend. Cool to lukewarm.

In a large mixing bowl dissolve the yeast in the warm water with the ½ teaspoon honey or sugar. When bubbly, add potato mixture, eggs and salt. Beat well.

Add 2½ cups of the flour and beat 2 minutes with an electric mixer or at least 200 strokes by hand. Stir in wheat germ. Gradually add enough more flour to make a dough that leaves the sides of the bowl. Turn the dough out onto a lightly floured board and knead until smooth and elastic. Add a little more flour as necessary. Put the dough in a buttered bowl; turn to coat all sides. Cover with a towel and let rise until it has doubled in size.

Punch the dough down, turn it out onto a lightly floured board, knead a few times to press out air bubbles, cut in half, cover with the towel, and let rest about 10 minutes.

Roll each half into a rectangle about ½ inch thick. It may be so elastic that it's hard to roll, but persist. Spread each half with 4-5 tablespoons soft butter and sprinkle with ½ to 1 cup chopped fresh herbs. I like a combination of dill, parsley and chives, but it's fun to experiment. If it's winter and you don't have herbs growing on your windowsill, try fresh parsley (widely available), freeze-dried chives, and dried basil. Or use just fresh parsley. If you're reduced to dried herbs, use only ¼ to ⅓ cup.

Now, start at the short end and roll dough up tightly, like a jelly roll. Place it in a buttered loaf pan, seam side down. The ends of the roll should touch the ends of the pan but the roll should not fill the pan much more than halfway. Repeat with the other piece of dough.

Brush the tops of the loaves with melted butter, cover and let rise in a warm place until almost doubled in size.

Preheat oven to 375°F. Bake about 40 minutes, or until the bottoms of the loaves sound hollow when tapped. Cool on a rack.

Makes two loaves. Eat one and freeze one for an herbal delight in some other season.

1 cup milk

½ cup sweet butter (1 stick)

1 cup warm mashed potatoes

3 tablespoons honey

1½ tablespoons dry yeast

½ cup warm water in which potatoes were cooked

½ teaspoon honey or sugar

2 eggs

1 tablespoon salt

6-7 cups unbleached white flour

¼ cup wheat germ (optional)

8-10 tablespoons soft butter

1-2 cups chopped fresh herbs

North African bread.

NORTH AFRICAN CORIANDER BREAD

This exotic bread puffs up like a mushroom and is subtly spicy.

In a sauce pan scald the milk. Add the butter and honey and allow to cool to lukewarm.

In a large mixing bowl combine the yeast with the warm water and ½ teaspoon sugar or honey. Let sit until bubbling. Add the milk mixture to the yeast, along with the eggs, salt, coriander, ginger, cinnamon, cloves, orange peel, and 3½ cups of the flour. Beat all together 2 minutes with an electric mixer or at least 200 strokes by hand. Gradually add about 3 cups more flour, or as much as it takes to form a dough that clings together and leaves the sides of the bowl. Turn the dough out onto a floured surface and knead until smooth and elastic, sprinkling with a little more flour if it remains too sticky. Try to maintain a dough of soft consistency.

Put the dough in a buttered bowl, turn it to coat or brush the top with melted butter, cover with a towel and let rise until doubled in bulk.

Punch the dough down, turn it out onto a lightly floured surface, knead a few times to press out air bubbles, cut in half, cover and let rest for about 10 minutes. Form the lumps of dough into two round balls. Grease two round pans (casseroles, soufflé dishes, or coffee cans). The capacity should be about 2 to 3 quarts and they can be shallow or deep, but a tall narrow pan will produce the most dramatic loaf. If, when you get the dough in the pan, it fills it much more than half-way, take it out and choose another pan. You can use two large loaf pans.

Place the balls of dough in the pans, brush the tops with melted butter, cover and let rise again until doubled, or almost doubled, in size.

Preheat oven to 350°F. Bake about 45 minutes, or until the bottoms sound hollow when tapped. It can be quite a trick to slide these loaves out of their pans to test, so be sure you're well armed with oven mitts.

If you like, about 10 minutes before you expect them to be done, brush the tops with a glaze of whole egg beaten with 2 tablespoons milk.

Carefully remove loaves from pans to cool on a rack.

Makes two round loaves.

1½ cups milk

½ cup sweet butter (1 stick) or light oil or a combination

½ cup honey

2 tablespoons dry yeast

½ cup warm water

½ teaspoon sugar or honey

2 eggs

2 teaspoons salt

1½ tablespoons ground coriander

¼ teaspoon ground ginger

½ teaspoon ground cinnamon

¼ teaspoon ground cloves

1 teaspoon grated orange peel

7 cups unbleached white flour, approximately (or substitute part whole wheat flour)

COTTAGE CHEESE BISCUITS

Light, good and another way to use cottage cheese.

1½ cups unbleached white flour

½ teaspoon salt

2 teaspoons baking powder

½ teaspoon baking soda

1 teaspoon sugar

6 tablespoons lard (or 3 tablespoons sweet butter and 3 tablespoons vegetable shortening). Whatever you use should be cold.

2 beaten eggs

⅔ cup small-curd cottage cheese

Sift together the flour, salt, baking powder, soda and sugar. Cut in the lard with a pastry blender or two knives, until evenly, coarsely textured. Mix together the eggs and cottage cheese, add to flour mixture and toss together with a fork.

Preheat the oven to 425°F. Turn the mixture out onto a floured board and gather it together with your hands. It won't want to cohere at first. Knead a few times (a pastry scraper is helpful for lifting and underneath) just until it holds together enough to roll. At this point the dough can be refrigerated, wrapped in wax paper, for 30 minutes or up to 24 hours, if you wish to delay baking.

Roll out with a rolling pin lightly dusted with flour, making sure the edges of the dough aren't sticking to the board, ¼–⅓-inch thick. Cut with a cookie cutter dipped in flour and lift each round with a spatula onto a baking sheet. Gather the scraps of dough, reroll and recut. Let the biscuits sit, lightly covered, for a few minutes or a couple of hours or overnight in the refrigerator.

Bake at 425°F. for 10 to 12 minutes or until lightly browned. Serve hot.

Makes about 14 biscuits.

ZUCCHINI CHEESE BREAD

This bread is moist, rich and has a unique flavor. It is not sweet. Serve warm from the oven. The slices, golden yellow with tiny flecks of green peel, are strangely attractive. If possible, it is even better toasted or sliced and lightly browned under the broiler. This makes a sensual accompaniment to a summer lunch or soup or salad.

2 eggs

¼ cup honey

2 tablespoons melted sweet butter

¾ cup sour cream

1¼ cups grated raw young zucchini, peel and all

2 cups unbleached white flour

½ teaspoon salt

2 teaspoons baking powder

½ teaspoon baking soda

½ cup grated Parmesan or cheddar cheese

Preheat oven to 350°F. Beat the eggs until light and slightly thick. Beat in the honey, melted butter and sour cream. Stir in the zucchini, mixing well.

Sift together the flour, salt, baking powder, and soda. Sprinkle the cheese over the flour and toss with a fork so that the cheese is well distributed.

Add the flour mixture to the zucchini mixture. Fold gently to mix.

Pour into a greased medium loaf pan and bake for 50-55 minutes or until the top feels springy. Let the bread sit in its pan for about 10 minutes before removing to cool on a rack.

BASQUE SHEPHERD'S BREAD

A friend who hand-carried a jar of prize sourdough starter from Oregon to the East Coast became engaged in conversation with a stranger on the plane. Eventually the stranger offered this recipe, which was copied down on the back of an envelope. I am grateful to the stranger and the friend. This is a very basic bread, with good texture and arresting sourness.

In a large glass, plastic or crockery bowl combine the starter, 1½ cups warm water and 2 cups white flour. Cover with plastic wrap and leave in a warm place overnight or up to 24 hours.

When you proceed, add the yeast, ¼ cup warm water, honey, salt and soft butter to the sponge and beat well. Add 2 cups of the remaining flour and beat with an electric mixer on medium speed for 2 minutes or at least 200 strokes by hand.

Add the rest of the flour gradually, stopping when the dough is stiff enough to pull away from the sides of the bowl.

Turn the dough out onto a floured surface and knead until smooth and elastic, adding a little more flour as necessary if it remains too sticky. Place the dough in a buttered bowl, turn it, or brush the top with melted butter. Cover with a damp kitchen towel and let rise until doubled in bulk.

Punch the dough down, turn out onto a lightly floured surface, knead a few times, divide into two pieces, cover, and let rest for 10-15 minutes. Form the pieces into two circular bubbles and place on a buttered baking sheet dusted with cornmeal. Brush the tops and sides of the loaves with melted butter, cover, and let rise again until almost doubled.

Preheat the oven to 350°F. Bake for about 45 minutes, or until the bottoms of the loaves sound hollow when tapped. About 10 minutes before they should be done, brush the loaves with a glaze of whole egg beaten with 2 tablespoons water or milk.

Cool on a rack.

The stranger directed that this bread be cut into wedges like a pie and served with seasoned sour cream. It's also fine with butter or cheese.

Makes two loaves.

1 cup sourdough starter
1½ cups warm water
2 cups unbleached white flour
½ tablespoon dry yeast
¼ cup warm water
¼ cup honey
1 tablespoon salt
5 tablespoons soft butter
4-5 cups whole wheat flour, or a combination of unbleached white and whole wheat
Egg for glaze

DANISH LOAF WITH ALMONDS AND KIRSCH

Elegant and sophisticated.

1½ cups unbleached white
  flour
 2 teaspoons baking
  powder
½ teaspoon salt
 2 eggs
½ cup honey
 1 teaspoon vanilla
¼ teaspoon almond extract
⅔ cup heavy cream
¾ cup ground almonds
  Sweet butter
 2 tablespoons Kirsch
 2 tablespoons granulated
  sugar

Preheat oven to 325°F.

Sift together the flour, baking powder and salt. In a mixing bowl beat the eggs until light and somewhat thickened. Beat in the honey, vanilla and almond extract.

In another bowl beat the heavy cream until it holds stiff peaks. Rub a medium loaf pan liberally with butter and dust the entire inside with ground almonds. Turn the pan upside down over the bowl in which you have beaten the eggs so excess almonds will fall into the batter, then stir in whatever almonds remain of the original ¾ cup. When well mixed, add the whipped cream and fold in gently. Then stir in the flour until just incorporated.

Pour the batter into the prepared pan and bake about 45 minutes or until the top feels springy. Remove pan from oven and punch holes with a cake tester all over the top, penetrating almost to the bottom of the pan.

In a small pan mix together the Kirsch and sugar and boil for about a minute. Spoon this all over the top of the loaf. Let the bread sit in the pan about 10 minutes before removing to cool on a rack. Try not to dislodge the bits of almond which have adhered to the sides and be sure to turn it top side up. Slice thinly and serve as a festive tea bread.

Makes one medium loaf.

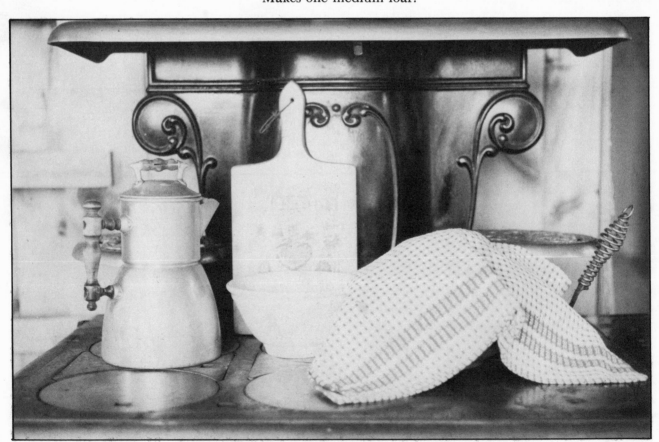

Bread rising on warm wood stove.

CRUSTY CHEESE BATTER BREAD

This bread is even better toasted, which accentuates the cheesy flavor.

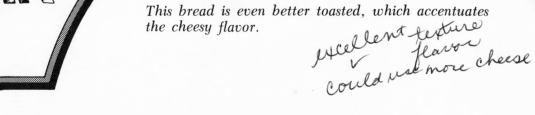

excellent texture / could use more cheese

In a saucepan scald the milk. Add the butter, honey, salt and grated cheese and let the mixture sit, after stirring well, until it is lukewarm. In a large bowl dissolve the yeast and teaspoon sugar or honey in the warm water. When bubbly, add the eggs and cooled milk mixture and beat.

Add about 3 cups flour and beat very thoroughly for 5 to 10 minutes. If time permits, cover the bowl and let the sponge swell for an hour or two. Stir it down and gradually add about 2½ cups more flour, beating or stirring until the dough pulls away from the sides of the bowl and holds together.

Cover the bowl and let the dough rise until it has doubled in size.

Stir down the dough and divide between two buttered 8×5-inch loaf pans (cutting it may be easier than pulling it apart). Spread the dough as evenly as you can. Let the dough rise, covered, until it reaches the tops of the pans. Preheat the oven to 375°F.

Bake about 25 minutes, then remove loaves from their pans and put them directly on the oven rack for a few minutes more, or until they sound hollow when thumped on the bottom.

Two medium loaves.

1¼ cups milk
2 tablespoons butter
2 tablespoons honey
2 teaspoons salt, or 1½ teaspoons if using fresh Parmesan
½ cup grated fresh Parmesan or sharp cheddar cheese, or a mixture
2 tablespoons dry yeast
1 teaspoon sugar or honey
½ cup warm water
2 eggs
5½ cups unbleached white flour, approximately

365 9-14 SLC

SUMMER MUFFINS

A recipe for any fruit in season. Strawberries, raspberries, blackberries and peacnes are a few that come to mind.

2 cups unbleached white
  flour
1 tablespoon baking
  powder
½ teaspoon cinnamon
½ teaspoon salt
1 cup fresh berries or fruit,
  chopped if large
2 eggs
6 tablespoons honey
½ cup milk
¼ cup melted sweet butter

Preheat the oven to 400°F.

Sift together the flour, baking powder, cinnamon and salt. Gently toss in the berries. In another bowl, beat the eggs until light and thick. Add honey, milk and melted butter, beating well after each addition. Combine flour and egg mixtures with a few swift strokes. Stop just before the flour is completely incorporated and while batter is still rough. Spoon the batter into buttered muffin tins, filling each ⅔ full. Bake for about 20 minutes.

Makes 12-14 medium muffins.

great

Martha sniffing her muffins.

PUMPERNICKEL

A darkly flavorful bread that is great for buffet suppers or picnics.

In a large mixing bowl stir the yeast into the 2 cups warm water, along with teaspoon sugar or honey. Let it sit until bubbly. In a saucepan heat together over low heat the vinegar, molasses, chocolate and butter, stirring until the butter and chocolate are melted. Let this cool to lukewarm.

Add the chocolate mixture to the yeast mixture, along with the salt, caraway seeds and fennel seeds. Beat to mix.

Add 2½ cups white flour and beat 2 minutes with an electric mixer or at least 200 strokes by hand. Add all the rye flour, stirring until the dough leaves the sides of the bowl. Turn the dough out onto a board dusted with a little of the remaining white flour and knead, sprinkling the dough with a little more white flour if it remains too sticky. Be patient; this dough takes longer than usual to become resilient and it's easy to add too much flour, in which case a dry bread is inevitable. Put the dough into a buttered bowl, turn it over or brush the top with melted butter, cover with a damp kitchen towel and let it rise until it has doubled in bulk.

Punch the dough down, turn it out onto the board, knead a few times to press out air bubbles, cut in half, cover with the towel and let it rest for 10 to 15 minutes.

Shape the pieces of dough into two long ovals. Place them on a greased baking sheet that has been dusted with cornmeal. With a sharp knife or razor blade make shallow slashes across the loaves, at right angles to the long axis, about 4 for each loaf.

Brush the tops with melted butter, cover and let them rise until almost doubled.

Preheat oven to 375°F. Bake about 30 to 35 minutes, or until the bottoms sound hollow when tapped.

During the baking blend the cornstarch and water in a small pan. Bring to a boil, stirring with a fork or wire whisk, then remove from heat. Take the loaves from the oven about 10 minutes before they should be done and brush the tops with the cornstarch mixture. Return to the oven. This makes a nice shiny finish. Don't overcook. Cool on a rack.

Makes two loaves.

2 tablespoons dry yeast
2 cups warm water
1 teaspoon sugar or honey
¼ cup cider vinegar
⅓ cup dark unsulphured molasses
2 1-oz. squares unsweetened chocolate
2 tablespoons sweet butter
1 tablespoon salt
1 tablespoon caraway seeds
1 teaspoon fennel seeds
3 cups unbleached white flour, approximately
3½ cups rye flour, preferably stone-ground
Cornmeal
1 teaspoon cornstarch
⅓ cup water

PSOMI

This fat Greek loaf is light, airy, and scented with sesame.

1½ cups warm water

1 tablespoon dry yeast

½ teaspoon sugar or honey

2 teaspoons salt

2 tablespoons honey

¼ cup sesame oil (if unavailable use another light oil and add ¼ cup sesame seeds to the dough)

2 cups unbleached white flour

2 cups stone-ground whole wheat flour, approximately

Egg for glaze

¼ cup sesame seeds for tops of loaves

In a large mixing bowl dissolve the yeast in ½ cup of the warm water with the ½ teaspoon sugar or honey. When it is frothing, add the other cup water, salt, honey, sesame oil, and 2 cups white flour. Beat with an electric mixer 2 minutes or at least 200 strokes by hand.

Cover the bowl with a damp towel and let the sponge sit for an hour or two, or until it is swollen and bubbly on top. Stir down the sponge and gradually add enough whole wheat flour to make a dough that clings together and leaves the sides of the bowl.

Turn the dough out onto a floured board and knead until smooth and elastic, adding a little more whole wheat flour if it remains too sticky.

Put the dough in a buttered bowl, turn it or brush the top with melted butter, cover with a towel and let rise until doubled in bulk.

Punch the dough down, turn out onto a lightly floured board, knead a few times to press out air bubbles, cut into two equal pieces, cover and let rest for about 10 minutes.

Grease a baking sheet and dust with cornmeal. Shape the pieces of dough into fat balls and press into thick pancakes, then tuck edges under, pinching together to seal and creating a smooth surface on top. Pat the dough with your hands to make a nice round.

Place the balls on the baking sheet, leaving plenty of space around them for expansion. Brush the tops with melted butter, cover with a light cloth and let rise again until almost doubled.

Preheat oven to 375°F. Bake for 20 minutes. Beat the egg well with a tablespoon water and get the sesame seeds ready in a saucer near the stove.

After 20 minutes remove the baking sheet from the oven. Brush one loaf all over with the egg glaze and immediately sprinkle two tablespoons sesame seeds over as much of the surface as possible (this is a liberal amount). Repeat with the other loaf.

Return loaves to the oven for another 5 minutes, or until the bottoms sound hollow when tapped. Cool on wire rack.

Makes two round loaves.

September

ANGEL BISCUITS

These have the light texture of a yeast bread but are as easy to bake as a quick bread.

1 tablespoon dry yeast

¼ cup warm water

½ teaspoon sugar or honey

2 cups unbleached white flour

2 teaspoons baking powder

1 tablespoon sugar

1 teaspoon salt

2 tablespoons sweet butter (cold)

1 tablespoon vegetable shortening (cold)

½ cup milk, at room temperature

Dissolve the yeast in the warm water with the ½ teaspoon sugar or honey. Let it sit until bubbly.

Sift together the flour, baking powder, tablespoon sugar and salt. Cut in the butter and shortening with a pastry blender or two knives. Mix the milk and yeast mixture together, then add to the flour. Toss with a fork, then turn out onto a floured board, gather together with your hands and knead gently a few times.

With a floured rolling pin roll out the dough ⅓-inch thick. Cut with a cookie cutter dipped in flour and remove the rounds with a spatula to a greased baking sheet. Gather up the scraps of dough on the board, roll out again and cut more biscuits. Let the biscuits rise, lightly covered, about an hour (or longer in the refrigerator).

Preheat the oven to 450°F. Bake about 10 minutes. Serve hot. This makes about sixteen 2½-inch biscuits.

CREAM AND HONEY WHOLE WHEAT BREAD

With the onset of autumn one waits to abandon the frivolities of summer for something more substantial. Like a 100 percent whole wheat bread. This one is rich, simple and good.

In a large mixing bowl dissolve the yeast in the warm water with the ½ teaspoon sugar or honey. Let it sit until frothing. Add the cream, honey, eggs and salt and beat well. Add 2 cups of the flour and beat with an electric mixer 2 minutes or at least 200 strokes by hand. If time permits, cover the bowl and let the sponge sit in a draft-free spot for an hour or two, until noticeably swollen. Stir it down and gradually add more flour, until the dough pulls away from the sides of the bowl.

Turn the dough out onto a floured board and knead until smooth and elastic, sprinkling with a little more flour if it remains too sticky. Expect this dough to remain somewhat clingy even after it is elastic. Don't add too much flour or you will end up with a dry loaf.

Put the dough into a buttered bowl, turn it over or brush the top with melted butter, cover with a damp kitchen towel and let rise until doubled in bulk.

Punch the dough down, turn it out onto the board, knead a few times to press out air bubbles, cut in half, cover with the towel and let it rest for 10-15 minutes.

Grease 2 medium loaf pans. Shape the dough into loaves and put in the pans. Brush the tops with melted butter, cover and let rise again until almost doubled in size. Preheat oven to 350°F. Bake about 30 minutes, or until the bottoms sound hollow when tapped. For a tender crust, brush the tops with melted butter when you take them from the oven. Cool on a rack.

Makes two medium loaves.

- 1½ tablespoons dry yeast
- ½ cup warm water
- ½ teaspoon sugar or honey
- 1 cup heavy cream, at room temperature
- ⅓-½ cup honey, according to preference
- 2 eggs
- 2 teaspoons salt
- 5 cups stone-ground whole wheat flour

Bee Hive

CIDER MUFFINS

delicious

The perfect thing for breakfast of a brisk morning.

2 cups unbleached white flour

1½ teaspoons baking powder

1 teaspoon baking soda

½ teaspoon salt

1 teaspoon cinnamon

⅔ cup raisins

1 egg

¾ cup fresh apple cider (not apple juice)

4 tablespoons melted sweet butter

¼ cup maple syrup

Cinnamon sugar:

3 tablespoons sugar or brown sugar mixed with 1 teaspoon cinnamon

Preheat the oven to 400°F.

Sift together the flour, baking powder, soda, salt and cinnamon. Toss in the raisins.

In another bowl beat the egg until light and slightly thickened. Add the cider, butter and maple syrup and beat to mix. Add the flour mixture and blend gently with a rubber spatula or wooden spoon, stopping just as the flour is incorporated and while the batter is still quite rough and lumpy. Spoon the batter into buttered muffin tins, filling about ⅔ full. Bake 20 minutes. Brush the tops with melted butter and sprinkle with cinnamon sugar. Serve hot.

Makes about 12 muffins.

Antique muffin tin.

POORIS

These Indian breads are crisp, air-filled puffs, scented with celery seed and poetic with a great many things besides curries.

These breads must be started well ahead of the meal. Sift together the white flour and salt. Mix in the whole wheat flour and celery seeds with a fork. Cut in the butter with a pastry blender or two knives. Add the yogurt and mix with a fork, then enough water to make a firm dough.

Turn out onto a lightly floured board and knead lightly a few times until the dough holds together. Wrap it in plastic or wax paper and let it rest in the refrigerator for 2 hours to 2 days.

Remove the dough and cut into 16 equal pieces. Form into balls with your hands and, one at a time, press to flatten slightly and then roll out on a lightly floured board with a floured rolling pin to a thin round about 3½ inches in diameter.

Don't worry if they are slightly irregular in shape. Place each round on a baking sheet as it is rolled so you can carry them all at once to the stove. Let them sit for 5 minutes.

In a wok or large heavy pan heat about 1½ inches of oil, preferably peanut oil, to 400°F. A candy thermometer is a great help here because the right temperature is critical. If you have one, leave it in the oil as you cook so you can constantly check the temperature. If you don't have one, just be sure the oil is quite hot; a tiny piece of dough thrown in should fizz instantly but not too furiously.

Take the rounds one at a time from the sheet with a wide egg turner and slide them into the oil. Remember, just one at a time. As you slide the poori in it will sink, then rise to the surface. Very gently prod the top with a slotted spoon to keep the bottom in good contact with the hot oil. If all goes well the top of the poori will almost immediately puff up like a balloon. As this happens cease touching it with the spoon. Let it fry until golden brown on the bottom, then turn it over with your spoon to brown the top side. The entire process only takes a minute or two. Remove the poori with the slotted spoon and drain on paper towels. Repeat with the remaining pooris. Serve them hot. Pooris which do not puff will be somewhat heavy but still have a good flavor.

This recipe makes 16.

1 cup unbleached white flour
½ teaspoon salt
½ cup whole wheat flour, preferably stone-ground
½ teaspoon celery seeds
1 tablespoon soft butter
¼ cup plain yogurt
⅓ cup water, approximately

CARROT CORN BREAD

This mellow bread is the color of turning leaves.

1 cup unbleached white flour

2 teaspoons baking powder

½ teaspoon salt

1 cup cornmeal, preferably stone-ground

2 eggs

2 tablespoons honey

2 tablespoons melted sweet butter

1 cup half and half or light cream

1½ cups shredded or grated carrots

Preheat the oven to 375°F. Sift together the flour, baking powder and salt. Mix in the cornmeal with a fork. Beat the eggs until they are light and slightly thickened. Add the honey and beat; beat in the melted butter and half and half. Stir in the carrots. Add the cornmeal mixture and blend lightly but thoroughly. Grease a 9-to 10-inch heavy skillet and heat it in the oven. Pour in the batter and bake until the center is firm, about 30 minutes. Cut into wedges and serve with butter. Leftovers can be split, buttered and toasted under the broiler.

Serves 10.

Corn bread.

INDIAN CORN BREAD

Pumpkin and blueberries are the secret ingredients in this colorful bread. Perhaps the Indians also knew a secret way to get them to ripen at the same time—you and I will probably resort to canned pumpkin or frozen blueberries.

Preheat the oven to 350°F.

Sift together the flour, baking powder and salt. Mix in the cornmeal with a fork. Gently toss in berries so all are coated with flour.

In another bowl beat the eggs until they are light in color and slightly thickened. Add the syrup or honey and beat, then the butter or oil, milk and pumpkin and beat to blend. Add the flour mixture and combine as gently as possible with a rubber spatula so as not to crush the berries.

Pour the batter into a large buttered loaf pan. Bake 50 to 55 minutes or until the top feels softly springy. Let sit in the pan for a few minutes before removing to a rack. Best served warm from the oven—or toast later under the broiler.

Makes one large loaf.

1 cup unbleached white flour

1 tablespoon baking powder

½ teaspoon salt

1 cup yellow cornmeal, preferably stone-ground

1 cup fresh blueberries, washed and well drained, or frozen blueberries, thawed and drained

2 eggs

¼ cup maple syrup or honey

¼ cup melted sweet butter or light oil

⅔ cup evaporated milk, half and half, or plain sweet milk

1 cup cooked mashed pumpkin or canned pumpkin

GREEN MOUNTAIN GREEN TOMATO BREAD

Northern gardeners often end the season with a plethora of unripe tomatoes, which happens to coincide with the first pressings of apple cider. Put them together and you have something strange and wonderful.

2¼ cups unbleached white flour

1½ teaspoons baking powder

1 teaspoon baking soda

½ teaspoon salt

¾ teaspoon ground cinnamon

½ teaspoon ground ginger

¼ cup minced crystallized ginger (optional)

2 eggs

⅓ cup maple syrup or honey

⅓ cup melted sweet butter or light oil or a combination

⅔ cup fresh apple cider

1-1¼ cups diced green tomatoes

¾ cup chopped walnuts

Preheat the oven to 325°F. Sift together the flour, baking powder, soda, salt, cinnamon and ginger. Toss in the crystallized ginger, if using, separating well.

In a large mixing bowl beat the eggs until they are light and slightly thickened. Add the maple syrup or honey and beat, then the butter and cider, beating to mix. Stir in the tomatoes and nuts. Add the dry ingredients and fold in gently until just combined. Pour the batter into a buttered large loaf pan and bake 55 to 60 minutes or until the top feels springy and the edges are browning. Let sit in the pan for about 10 minutes before removing to cool on a rack.

Makes one loaf.

NANCY LIVERMORE'S CINNAMON SWIRL

This works well with any basic white or whole wheat recipe, such as the Cream and Honey Whole Wheat Bread. In a two-loaf recipe, make one plain and the other fancy, with the filling below.

Take the dough for one loaf, after its first rise. Roll it out on a lightly floured board into a rectangle ⅓-inch thick. Blend butter and spices together with a fork. Spread this evenly over the dough. Sprinkle on nuts and raisins.

Roll up the dough tightly from one of the short ends and place in a greased loaf pan or on a buttered baking sheet, seam side down. Use a pan a size larger than the one for a plain loaf from the same recipe. If using a baking sheet, pinch the ends of the dough together so the filling won't fall out. Brush the top with melted butter and let rise and bake according to the recipe.

If you have used the larger amount of butter you may find a small melted pool in the bottom of the pan when you remove the baked loaf. In this case, place the loaf directly on the oven rack for a couple of minutes to let the crust dry out.

Filling:

- 4-6 tablespoons soft sweet butter
- 2 teaspoons ground cinnamon
- ½ teaspoon ground nutmeg
- ¼ teaspoon cardamon or mace
- ½ cup finely chopped or ground nuts
- ⅓-½ cup raisins

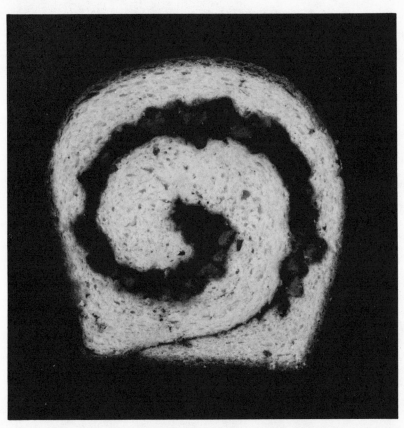

Cinnamon swirl bread with nuts and raisins.

CRUNCHY BATTER BREAD

This has a closer texture than most and is full of healthful things.

1½ teaspoons dry yeast

½ cup warm water

½ teaspoon honey or sugar

1 13-oz. can evaporated milk

3 tablespoons honey

¼ teaspoon ginger

1 teaspoon salt

2 tablespoons melted butter or light oil

3 cups unbleached white flour

1 cup stone-ground whole wheat flour

½ cup wheat germ

¼ cup cracked wheat or bulgur

In a large bowl dissolve the yeast in the warm water with ½ teaspoon sugar or honey. Let it sit until bubbling, then add the evaporated milk, 3 tablespoons honey, ginger, salt, butter, and 3 cups white flour. Beat very thoroughly for 5 to 10 minutes. Add the whole wheat flour, wheat germ and cracked wheat, beating all the time. If the dough doesn't yet leave the sides of the bowl and form a cohesive mass, add a little more white flour. Let the dough rise in its bowl, covered with a towel, until it has doubled in size. Stir down the dough with a wooden spoon and divide equally between two well-buttered 1-lb. coffee cans. Butter the insides of the lids and place on the cans. Let the dough rise until the lids come off the cans. There may be a resounding pop or they may just ooze off.

Preheat the oven to 350°F. When the lids come off, bake the breads for 45 minutes. It's difficult to test this bread for doneness so it's especially important to have an accurate oven thermometer.

While baking, the dough will puff out over the tops like two tall mushrooms. Let the breads cool in their cans for 5 to 10 minutes on a rack before sliding them out. If they don't slide out readily, grasp them gently with a towel by the mushroom top and pull. Finish cooling on a rack.

Makes two tall loaves.

Kneading dough outside means not having to worry about flour on the floor.

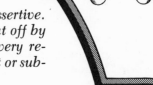

SOURDOUGH RYE BREAD

This is a richly evocative bread, tart and spicy but not too assertive. Fine for a hike or picnic with cheese and fruit. Don't be put off by the multiple ingredients; the making of this loaf can be very relaxed. If you don't have something in the recipe, leave it out or substitute. Improvisation is the mother of inspiration.

In a large plastic, glass or crockery bowl, mix together the starter, ½ cup each rye and white flours and ½ cup warm water. If the batter seems too stiff to beat together easily add a little more water. Cover with plastic wrap and let sit 6 hours or overnight.

Add to the bowl the yeast, ½ cup warm water, honey or maple syrup, mashed potatoes, and 1 cup each of rye and white flours. Mix and let stand again, covered with plastic, at least 6 hours or until the next day. Add the oil, salt, fennel, caraway seeds, orange peel, molasses, 2 cups rye flour and 2 cups white flour, stirring until the dough is too stiff to mix further by hand. Turn the dough out onto a floured board and knead until smooth and elastic, adding a little more white flour if the dough remains persistently sticky. Resist the impulse to add too much too soon or you will have a dry bread. Put the dough into a buttered bowl, brush the top with melted butter, cover with a damp towel and let rise until doubled in bulk. Punch the dough down, turn out onto a lightly floured surface, knead a few times to press out air bubbles, divide in half, cover and let rest for about 10 minutes.

Grease a cookie sheet and dust with cornmeal. Shape the balls of dough into two oval or round shapes, put on the sheet and brush the tops with melted butter. With a sharp knife slash a cross or other design in the tops of the loaves, about ¼-inch deep. Cover again with the towel and let rise until almost doubled. Preheat the oven to 425°F. Bake for 15 minutes. During this time you can mist or brush the loaves with cold water two or three times for a hard crust. Reduce the heat to 350°F. and bake an additional 15 to 20 minutes, or until the bottoms sound hollow when tapped. Cool on a rack. Slice thinly.

Makes two loaves.

- 1 cup sourdough starter
- ½ cup rye flour, preferably stone-ground
- ½ cup unbleached white flour
- ½ cup warm water
- 1 tablespoon dry yeast
- ½ cup warm water
- 2 tablespoons honey or maple syrup
- ½ cup mashed potatoes
- 1 cup rye flour, preferably stone-ground
- 1 cup unbleached white flour
- 2 tablespoons light oil
- 2 teaspoons salt
- 2 teaspoons fennel seeds
- 1 teaspoon caraway seeds
- ½ teaspoon grated orange peel
- ¼ cup unsulphured molasses
- 2 cups rye flour, preferably stone-ground
- 2-3 cups unbleached white flour

CINNAMON TWISTS

These light, crunchy and spicy rolls have nothing to recommend them except sensual adventure. The kind of thing where you surreptitiously devour the crumbs left on the baking sheet . . . while they're still so hot they burn your tongue.

½ cup sweet butter
  (1 stick)

2 tablespoons honey

1 teaspoon salt

¼ cup milk

1 teaspoon vanilla

1 tablespoon plus
  1 teaspoon dry yeast

¼ cup warm water

½ teaspoon sugar or
  honey

1½ cups unbleached
  white flour

3 eggs

1½-1¾ cups unbleached
  white flour

1 cup granulated or
  raw sugar

1 cup ground or very
  finely chopped nuts

2 tablespoons ground
  cinnamon

Melted butter

In a small saucepan heat together the butter, honey, salt and milk until the butter has melted. Remove from heat and let cool to lukewarm. Stir in the vanilla.

In a large mixing bowl dissolve the yeast in the warm water with the ½ teaspoon sugar or honey. When bubbly, add the butter mixture and 1½ cups flour. Beat 2 minutes with an electric mixer or 200 strokes by hand. Cover and let rest for 15 minutes to an hour.

Beat in the eggs one at a time, then 1½ cups more flour. The dough will be very soft; if it is too runny to hold together you can add another ¼ cup flour.

Turn the dough out onto a floured board (dig it out with hands dipped in flour) and knead or work it around for 5 minutes. Submit to its clinginess and don't add more flour unless it's absolutely impossible. Use a pastry scraper to help lift it off the board.

Rub some flour into a soft linen dish towel or other tightly woven cloth. Put the dough in the middle of the towel and tie the ends of the towel together, enclosing the lump of dough but leaving room for it to expand to double its present size. Don't worry about openings in the folds of cloth—the dough is going to get wet anyway.

Fill a very large bowl or pot with warm water—85° to 100°F. Not more than 105°F., however. Use a thermometer. Plunk the towel-wrapped dough right into the bowl. It will sink. Now go about your business. Check the thermometer every now and then and add some hot water to the bowl as it cools. When the dough rises above the water and is very soft and puffy, it's ready.

Hold the towel over the sink to let it drain a bit, then unwrap the dough and scrape it out onto a floured board. Dip your hands in flour and knead a few times. Cover with a dry towel.

In a bowl mix together the sugar, ground nuts and cinnamon. Put your pan of melted butter nearby. Cut off pieces of the dough (count on 20 to 22 equal-sized pieces). Press each piece into a somewhat flattened strip about 5 inches long. Don't worry about the exact shape. Brush the strip with melted butter or dip it into the pan. Then roll it in the bowl of cinnamon-sugar-nuts, making sure it gets well coated all over. Twist the strip into a circle with both ends overlapping, or any other shape that takes your fancy. Place on a buttered baking sheet. Leave room for expansion; it will take two sheets. Let the rolls sit for 15 minutes to an hour, until they are somewhat swollen.

Preheat the oven to 375°F.

Bake about 15 minutes. Remove and cool on racks, if not serving right away. You now have a feast of toasted cinnamon bits on the baking sheets, not to mention the funny looking twist or two that really should be eaten just to get rid of it.

Makes 20 to 22 twists.

October

CHEESE BREAD

This is really cheesy and makes sensational toast. It benefits from three risings.

1 cup milk
1 tablespoon sweet butter
¼ cup honey
1 tablespoon dry yeast
¼ cup warm water
½ teaspoon sugar or honey
1½ teaspoons salt
1 egg
4 cups unbleached white flour, approximately
2 cups sharp chedder cheese, grated

Scald the milk in a small saucepan; add the butter and honey and let it sit until lukewarm. In a large mixing bowl dissolve the yeast in the warm water with the ½ teaspoon sugar or honey. Wait until it is frothing. Add the lukewarm milk to the yeast, along with the salt and egg; beat all together. Add 1½ cups of the flour and beat 2 minutes with an electric mixer or at least 200 strokes by hand. Mix in the cheese and gradually add more flour until the dough leaves the sides of the bowl and is stiff enough to knead.

Turn the dough out onto a floured board and knead until smooth and elastic, sprinkling with a little more flour if it remains sticky. Put the dough in a buttered bowl, turn it over or brush the top with melted butter, cover with a towel and let rise until double in size. Punch it down in the bowl and, if you have time, allow it to rise again. (It will rise faster this time.)

Grease an oval or round casserole and shape the dough to fit. The dough should fill half the pan. Put in the pan, brush the top with melted butter, cover with the towel and let rise again until almost double.

You can preheat the oven to 350°F. or put this bread in a cold oven, turn it on to 350°, bake 40 to 45 minutes and then take the bread out of the pan and put it directly on the oven rack for a final 5 minutes. It is done when the bottom sounds hollow when tapped. Cool on a rack.

Makes one large loaf.

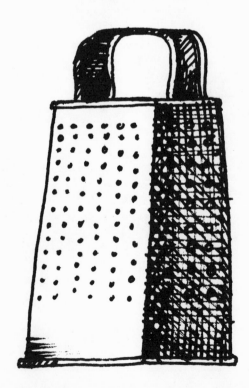

PERSIMMON BREAD

Persimmons taste unlike anything else on God's earth. If you're lucky enough to live where you can get the small dark homely wild ones, use those; otherwise the large orange beautiful ones in the market will do, though persimmons prove the homily that beauty is only skin deep.

Preheat oven to 350°F.

Sift together the flour, baking powder, soda, salt and spices. In a mixing bowl beat the eggs until they are light and somewhat thickened. Beat in the honey, then the melted butter, lastly the persimmons.

Add the dry ingredients to the wet and fold in gently until just mixed. If the persimmon pulp was very moist and the batter seems too runny, sift in another 2 to 4 tablespoons flour and blend gently.

Pour the batter into a greased medium loaf pan. Bake about 45 minutes or until the top feels springy. Don't overcook. Let the loaf sit in the pan for about 10 minutes before removing to cool on a rack.

Makes one loaf.

2 cups unbleached white flour

2 teaspoons baking powder

½ teaspoon baking soda

½ teaspoon salt

½ teaspoon cinnamon

¼ teaspoon nutmeg

¼ teaspoon allspice

2 eggs

⅓ cup honey or maple syrup

¼ cup melted sweet butter or light oil or a combination

1 cup mashed persimmon pulp

Farmhouse coffeecake.

FARMHOUSE COFFEECAKE

A rich filled bread.

Use the recipe for Farmhouse Bread (page 157). Use ½ cup honey. After the dough has risen once, punch it down, turn out onto a slightly floured board and cut in half. Cover and let rest about 10 minutes. Wrap one-half in the towel, press the other half to flatten and then roll out with a rolling pin into a more or less regular rectangle about ¼-inch thick. Spread the rectangle with:

4–6 tablespoons soft butter

Sprinkle all over with:

½ cup brown sugar
⅔ cup gold raisins, approximately
¾ cup chopped nuts, approximately

Roll the dough up like a jelly roll, starting with a long edge. Put the seam underneath and form into a large crescent or a doughnut shape, pinching the ends together to seal them. With a sharp knife make slashes all the way around the outside at about 2-inch intervals to give the dough room to expand. Put the dough on a large buttered baking sheet and brush top with melted butter.

Repeat this process with the other piece of dough, placing on a second baking sheet. Cover the rolls and let them rise until not quite doubled.

Preheat the oven to 400°F. Brush the tops of the coffeecakes with an egg white beaten with a tablespoon of water. Bake 30 minutes. With pancake turners remove to a rack. Serve warm. They may be reheated, wrapped in foil, or frozen for future use.

Makes two coffee rings.

SOURDOUGH CORN BREAD

This recipe does not call for a sponge to be set in advance, but, if you have time, the starter, cornmeal and milk may be mixed and allowed to sit for an hour or so. You will find that sourdough corn bread is rich and mellow, though somewhat coarser in texture than regular corn breads. Leftovers can be split and toasted with butter for another meal.

1 cup sourdough starter

1½ cups yellow cornmeal, preferably stone-ground

1½ cups cream, evaporated milk, buttermilk or sweet milk (a favored combination is 1 cup cream and ½ cup buttermilk)

2 eggs, beaten until light and thick

2 tablespoons maple syrup or honey

¼ cup melted butter (½ stick)

½ cup unbleached white flour

2 teaspoons salt

½ teaspoon baking powder

½ teaspoon baking soda

Mix together the starter, cornmeal and milk. Let sit for an hour or more. Add the eggs, maple syrup and melted butter (not too hot). Sift together the flour, salt, baking powder and soda. Stir in.

Preheat the oven to 425°F. Pour the batter into a greased 10-inch cast-iron frying pan or other heavy pan of the same capacity and bake for 30 minutes or until the middle is set. Serve in wedges with butter and honey, unless you are feeling austere, in which case it will more than suffice by itself.

HONEY AND BEER
WHOLE WHEAT BREAD

*Reminiscent of sourdough in its tangy flavor,
but with a finer texture.*

Heat the beer until it's warm (not over 110°F.). Pour it into a large mixing bowl and stir in the 1 teaspoon sugar or honey and the yeast. Let it sit until the yeast has dissolved and is bubbly.

Add the oil, honey, and salt. Add the 2 cups white flour and beat 2 minutes with an electric mixer or at least 200 strokes by hand. Gradually add 3 cups whole wheat flour or as much as it takes to form a dough that pulls away from the sides of the bowl. Turn the dough out onto a floured board and knead, sprinkling on a little more whole wheat flour if necessary, until the dough is smooth and elastic. If it remains slightly clingy, never mind; the important thing is that it be resilient.

Put the dough into a buttered bowl, turn it over or brush the top with melted butter, cover with a damp kitchen towel and let it rise until doubled in size.

Punch the dough down, turn it out onto the board, knead it a few times to press out air bubbles, cut in half, cover and let it rest for 10 to 15 minutes.

Grease 2 small to medium loaf pans. Shape the pieces of dough into loaves, put in pans and brush the tops with melted butter or make free-form ovals and place on a buttered baking sheet dusted with cornmeal. Cover with the towel and let the loaves rise again until about doubled in size.

Preheat oven to 350°F. Bake 30 to 40 minutes, or until the bottoms of the loaves sound hollow when tapped. Cool on a rack.

Makes two loaves.

1½ cups beer or ale
    (1 12-oz. can)
 1 teaspoon sugar or honey
1½ tablespoons dry yeast
 ¼ cup light oil
 ⅓ cup honey
 2 teaspoons salt
 2 cups unbleached white
    flour
3½ cups whole wheat flour,
    approximately, prefer-
    ably stone-ground

Freshly baked loaves cooling in a shop in Maine.

FARMHOUSE POTATO BREAD

•

To my mind, this is the definitive white bread, redolent of things which were found in abundance in an old-time farm kitchen (a prosperous one, I might add): milk, eggs, butter and honey. The use of potatoes is also traditional among American farm wives. This bread is very rich, but light, has a golden brown crust all over and makes wonderful toast. The degree of sweetness can be adjusted to your taste. It is also a versatile dough which adapts well to use for rolls, coffee cake and braids.

Celebrate coming inside for the winter. Even if you didn't have a garden, this bread can be your harvest.

1 cup milk
½ cup sweet butter (1 stick)
1 cup warm mashed potatoes
⅓-½ cup honey
1½ tablespoons dry yeast
½ cup warm water, preferably water in which potatoes have been cooked
½ teaspoon honey or sugar
¼ teaspoon ginger
2 eggs
2 teaspoons salt
6-7 cups unbleached white flour
¼ cup wheat germ (optional)
1 egg (for the glaze)

In a large saucepan bring the milk just to a boil. Turn off the heat and add the butter, mashed potatoes and honey, stirring vigorously with a wire whisk to blend. Let sit until it has cooled to lukewarm.

In a large mixing bowl dissolve the yeast in the warm water with the ½ teaspoon honey or sugar. Let it sit until frothing.

Add the lukewarm potato mixture to the yeast, along with the ginger, eggs and salt, and beat well.

Add 2½ cups of the flour and beat 2 minutes with an electric mixer or at least 200 strokes by hand. Stir in the wheat germ, if using. Gradually add more flour, as much as it takes to make a dough that leaves the sides of the bowl. Turn the dough out onto a lightly floured board and knead until smooth and elastic. Sprinkle on a little more flour if it remains insistently sticky, but expect some stickiness because of the potatoes. When it has become elastic, especially if blisters appear on the surface, you can stop kneading.

Put the dough in a buttered bowl, turn it over or brush the top with melted butter, cover with a kitchen towel and let rise until it has doubled in size.

Punch the dough down, turn it out onto the board, knead a few times to press out air bubbles, cut in half, cover with the towel and let rest about 10 minutes.

Grease two medium to large loaf pans. Shape the dough into loaves, put in pans, brush the tops with melted butter, cover and let rise again until about double in size.

Preheat oven to 375°F. Bake for 35 minutes. About 5 minutes before you expect them to be done, take the loaves out and brush with an egg beaten with 2 tablespoons milk or cream. They are done when the bottoms sound hollow when tapped. Remove from pans to cool on a rack.

Makes two loaves.

GRANOLA BATTER BREAD

2 tablespoons dry yeast

½ cup warm water

1 teaspoon sugar or honey

1 cup water

2 tablespoons sweet butter, soft or melted

2 tablespoons honey

1½ teaspoons salt

1 egg

3½–4 cups unbleached white flour

1½ cups granola, homemade or the freshest you can buy

In a large bowl dissolve the yeast in the ½-cup warm water with the teaspoon sugar or honey. When it is bubbly, add the cup water, butter, honey, salt and egg and beat well. Add 2½ cups flour and beat very thoroughly for 5 to 10 minutes. Stir in the granola. Gradually add about 1½ cups more flour or until the dough is too stiff to stir and gathers together in the middle of the bowl.

Let it rise in its bowl, covered with a towel, until double in size. Stir down with a wooden spoon and turn into one large, buttered loaf pan or two smaller ones; in either case the dough should fill the pan half-way. Cover and let rise again until the dough reaches the top of the pan(s).

Preheat the oven to 350°F.

Bake about 30 minutes for smaller loaves, 40 to 45 for one large loaf, or until it tests done. Remove loaves from the pan(s) and place directly on oven rack for another couple of minutes to crisp the crust. Cool on a rack if not eating immediately.

Makes one large or two small loaves.

SWEET POTATO CORN BREAD

Light, fluffy and rich but not noticeably sweet.

1 cup unbleached white flour

1 teaspoon baking powder

½ teaspoon baking soda

½ teaspoon salt

⅛ teaspoon allspice

pinch of mace

½ cup yellow cornmeal, preferably stone-ground

2 eggs

1 cup mashed sweet potatoes

4 tablespoons melted sweet butter or light oil

3 tablespoons maple syrup or honey

½ cup buttermilk or sour milk

½ teaspoon grated orange peel (optional)

Preheat the oven to 375°F.

Sift together the flour, baking powder, soda, salt, allspice and mace. Stir in the cornmeal with a fork.

In another bowl beat the eggs until light in color and thick. Add the sweet potatoes, melted butter, maple syrup, buttermilk and orange peel and beat to mix. Blend in the flour-meal mixture with a rubber spatula or wooden spoon.

Pour the batter into a buttered 8-inch skillet or square pan and bake 30 minutes or until the middle is set.

Serves 6.

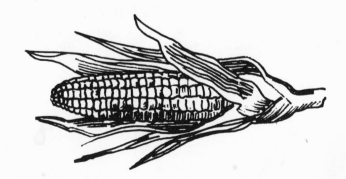

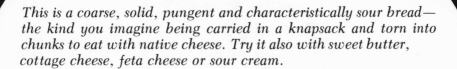

SOURDOUGH PUMPERNICKEL

•

*This is a coarse, solid, pungent and characteristically sour bread—
the kind you imagine being carried in a knapsack and torn into
chunks to eat with native cheese. Try it also with sweet butter,
cottage cheese, feta cheese or sour cream.*

Mix together the starter, molasses, potato water and 2 cups whole wheat flour in a large glass, plastic or crockery bowl. Cover with plastic wrap and let sit in a warm place overnight or as long as 24 hours. Heat the 1 cup water to boiling and pour over the cornmeal in a bowl, stirring energetically with a wire whisk until mixed and it thickens slightly. Stir in the mashed potatoes and blend well. Let this cool to lukewarm, then add to the starter mixture, along with the yeast, salt, oil and caraway seeds. Beat well.

Gradually add the 1 cup whole wheat and 4 cups rye flour, stirring until the dough pulls away from the sides of the bowl. If this doesn't happen add white flour.

Turn the dough out onto a floured board and knead until smooth and elastic, adding a little more white flour if it remains too sticky. Be patient; the low gluten content of the rye flour, along with the inherent stickiness of the potatoes, makes this an unrewarding matter in the dough stage. When the dough reaches a condition of resiliency, even if it is still a bit sticky you can stop kneading.

Place the dough in a buttered bowl, turn over or brush the top with melted butter, cover with a damp towel and let rise until doubled in bulk. Punch the dough down, turn out onto a lightly floured surface, knead a few times, divide in two, cover and let rest for 10 to 15 minutes. Shape into two round or oval free-form loaves and put on a buttered baking sheet which has been dusted with cornmeal. With a razor or knife make slashes in the tops of the loaves, about ¼-inch deep, perhaps a tic-tac-toe pattern for a round loaf or four straight crosswise slashes on a long oval loaf. Brush the tops with melted butter. Let rise again, covered with the towel, until almost doubled.

Have the oven preheated to 350°F. Bake 50 minutes or until the bottoms sound hollow when tapped. Ten minutes before you expect it to be done brush with a glaze of egg white beaten slightly with a tablespoon water. Cool on racks.

This makes two large loaves.

1 cup sourdough starter
¼ cup molasses
¾ cup potato water (water in which potatoes have been cooked)
2 cups whole wheat flour, preferably stone-ground
1 cup water
¼ cup yellow cornmeal
1 cup mashed potatoes
1 tablespoon dry yeast
1 tablespoon salt
2 tablespoons light oil
1 tablespoon caraway seeds
1 cup whole wheat flour, preferably stone-ground
4 cups rye flour, preferably stone-ground
1–2 cups unbleached white flour
Egg white for glaze

APPLE BREAD WITH CIDER

The apotheosis of autumn.

2 eggs

⅓ cup maple syrup or honey

½ cup melted sweet butter (1 stick) or light oil or a combination

½ cup apple cider

½ teaspoon vanilla

2 tablespoons applejack or calvados (optional—if omitting, increase cider by 2 tablespoons)

1½ cups finely chopped or grated tart apples (peel and all if they are well washed)

¾ cup chopped walnuts or pecans

2¼ cups unbleached white flour

2 teaspoons baking powder

½ teaspoon baking soda

½ teaspoon salt

½ teaspoon nutmeg

1 teaspoon cinnamon

¼ teaspoon allspice

Preheat oven to 325°F. In a mixing bowl beat the eggs until light or slightly thick. Add the maple syrup or honey and beat, then the melted butter, apple cider, vanilla and applejack and beat once more. Stir in the apples and nuts. Sift together the flour, baking powder, soda, salt, nutmeg, cinnamon and allspice. Stir the flour mixture into the batter, mixing just until combined. Pour into greased large loaf pan and bake 50 to 60 minutes or until the top feels springy. Let the loaf sit in its pan for 10 to 15 minutes before removing to cool on a rack.

Makes 1 loaf.

Counter-clockwise from top: Apple cider, fresh apple bread, apple sauce, apple butter, apple cobbler and apples.

SCOTTISH BAPS

Bearing one of those inimitable Anglo-Saxon names, these traditional country buns can be served with any meal or tea. Marmalade is an excellent accompaniment.

1½ cups milk

6 tablespoons butter, light oil, or a mixture

2 tablespoons honey

1 teaspoon salt

¼ cup warm water

1 tablespoon dry yeast

½ teaspoon sugar or honey

4 cups unbleached white flour, approximately

In a saucepan scald the milk. Add the butter, honey and salt and let sit until lukewarm.

In a large bowl dissolve the yeast in the warm water with the ½ teaspoon sugar or honey. When it is bubbling, add the cooled milk mixture and 2 cups of the flour. Beat with an electric mixer 2 minutes or at least 200 strokes by hand. Gradually add 2 cups more flour, or enough to make a kneadable dough. Turn the dough out onto a floured board and knead until smooth and elastic, sprinkling with a little more flour if it remains sticky. Put the dough in a buttered bowl, turn it to coat all sides or brush the top with melted butter, cover with a cloth and let rise until doubled in bulk.

Punch the dough down and turn out onto a lightly floured board. Knead a few times to press out air bubbles, cut into 16 equal pieces, cover and let rest for about 10 minutes. Shape each piece into a ball, press it gently with your hand to flatten slightly and roll it gently with a floured rolling pin to make a rather thin oval between 3 and 4 inches long. Lift the ovals onto baking sheets which you have first dusted with flour. Do not brush the tops with butter. Cover them with a light cloth and let rise until not quite doubled in size.

Preheat the oven to 400°F. Before baking, brush the tops of the buns with milk and sift a little flour over them. Bake 15 to 20 minutes. Cool on a rack if not eating immediately. They can be reheated later in foil, or split and toasted.

Makes 16 baps. Call up 15 friends and tell them you're going to serve baps. They won't believe it till they see them.

TOADS

Something like sweetish hushpuppies, these little breads doubtless derived their name from the bizarre shapes they assume when dropped into hot fat. Make these grotesqueries for Halloween or any other time you are feeling mischievous.

1 cup unbleached white flour

¼ teaspoon salt

¼ teaspoon baking soda

2 teaspoons baking powder

1 cup cornmeal, preferably stone-ground

1 egg

1 cup milk

2 tablespoons unsulphured molasses

2 tablespoons honey

Sift together the flour, salt, baking soda and baking powder. Add the cornmeal and stir to mix thoroughly with a fork.

In another bowl beat the egg, add the milk, molasses and honey and beat again. Stir in the flour mixture. The batter should be of a soft consistency but stiff enough to hold its shape on a spoon, or at least not to fall off the spoon. If it seems too thin, let it sit a while as the cornmeal will absorb moisture. If it is already stiff, add a little more milk.

Have ready some deep cooking oil in an even deeper pot, preheated to 375°–400°F. Use a candy thermometer if you have one and keep it in the pot so you can maintain the right temperature. Take a spoonful of the batter (heaping teaspoon or soup spoon) and, using another spoon to push it off, drop it into the fat. Don't worry about the shape of your spoonful as it will "explode" into an outlandish form when it hits the oil.

Cook only a few at a time, frying until they are quite brown and crisp all over. One problem is that because the oil is so hot they may become too dark before they are cooked through; this is the reason for using a not-too-large spoonful.

Remove the toads with a slotted spoon and drain on paper towels. Break open one of the first ones with a fork to see if it's done inside, but not done to the point of absolute dryness. If the toads brown too quickly you may have to turn down the heat a bit. Go slowly with the first few until you've got the right balance.

Serve while hot. They have a certain primitive appeal—crisp, grainy and sweet.

This makes anywhere from 18 to 24.

November

SOURDOUGH PRUNE NUT BREAD

This is a quick bread in that it is unkneaded, but the flavor is enhanced if the sponge can be made up in advance. It is open-textured, moist and fruity, and has that unmistakable sourdough tang.

1 cup sourdough starter

1 cup evaporated milk (or sweet milk or half and half)

1½ cups unbleached white flour

¼ cup melted butter

½ cup maple syrup or honey

1 egg, slightly beaten

1 cup pitted, chopped prunes

1 cup chopped nuts

1 cup unbleached white flour

1 teaspoon salt

½ teaspoon baking soda

1 teaspoon baking powder

In a large glass, crockery or plastic bowl mix together the starter, evaporated milk and flour. If possible, cover with plastic wrap and let sit 6 to 8 hours or overnight.

Add to the bowl the melted butter (not too hot), maple syrup, egg, prunes and nuts. Mix well.

Sift together the flour, salt, soda and baking powder. Stir into the liquid ingredients until just mixed. If the batter seems too liquid (wetter than a wet pudding), add ¼ cup more flour. Because of differences in starters and degree of fermentation in the sponge, one can't be precise about the amount of flour.

Preheat oven to 350°F. Pour the batter into two small to medium loaf pans and bake 40 to 45 minutes in their pans before removing to finish cooling on racks.

Slice thinly and serve with soft butter or cream cheese.

Makes two loaves.

SWEET SPICED CORN BREAD

1½ cups unbleached white flour

1 tablespoon baking powder

½ teaspoon salt

¼ teaspoon cinnamon

¼ teaspoon nutmeg

2 cups cornmeal, preferably stone-ground

½ cup gold raisins (optional)

4 eggs

½ cup honey or maple syrup

6 tablespoons melted sweet butter

1 cup milk

1 teaspoon grated orange peel

Preheat the oven to 400°F. Sift together the flour, baking powder, salt, cinnamon and nutmeg. Stir in the cornmeal with a fork. Toss in the raisins, if using.

In another bowl beat the eggs until they are light colored and slightly thick. Add the honey and beat, then the melted butter, milk and orange peel and beat to mix. Add the cornmeal mixture and blend in with a rubber spatula or wooden spoon.

Bake in a large buttered skillet or shallow casserole for 30 minutes or until the center is set.

Serves 12.

OWENDAW

A kind of spoon bread made with grits, owendaw is a rich, light and very old Southern concoction—simultaneously smooth and crunchy. Grits are probably one of the most disdained foods on God's earth—by non-Southerners, that is. Given a fair chance to acquaint themselves with this ingratiating grain, some people will still never understand. Some will.

Preheat the oven to 400°F. In a large bowl beat the eggs until they are light in color and thickened. Add the butter to the grits and stir to melt. Add the milk and buttermilk and beat with a wire whisk to make a smooth gruel. Sprinkle the salt, baking powder and soda over the cornmeal and mix thoroughly with a fork.

Pour grits mixture into the eggs and beat until smooth—be sure there aren't any lumps hiding in the bottom. Add the cornmeal and beat again briefly. If the batter seems very liquid, mix in a little more cornmeal; it should be a loose batter, however.

Butter a casserole or ovenproof dish (2½ to 3 qts.) Pour in the batter and bake about an hour or until the middle is set but still soft and the top golden brown. Dish it out with a spoon and serve with a pat of butter melting luxuriously on top.

Variation: Add ½ to 1 cup grated Swiss or cheddar cheese to the hot grits at the same time as the butter.

Serves 8.

4 eggs

4 tablespoons sweet butter

2½ cups hot cooked grits (about ½ cup raw grits cooked in 2½ cups water without salt)

1 cup milk

1 cup buttermilk or sour milk

2 teaspoons salt

2 teaspoons baking powder

1 teaspoon baking soda

1 cup cornmeal, preferably stone-ground

WALNUT OATMEAL BREAD

Oats and molasses have an affinity for each other; likewise oats and walnuts, walnuts and molasses, milk and honey. All are in rapport here.

1 cup water
1 cup milk
1 cup rolled oats
2 tablespoons sweet butter or light oil
2 teaspoons salt
¼ cup unsulphured molasses
¼ cup honey
1 tablespoon dry yeast
½ cup warm water
½ teaspoon sugar or honey
5½ unbleached white flour, approximately
¾ cup chopped walnuts

In a saucepan scald the milk with the water. Pour over the oats in a bowl and stir in the butter, salt, molasses and honey. Let this cool to lukewarm.

In a large mixing bowl dissolve the yeast in the ½ cup warm water with the ½ teaspoon sugar or honey. When frothing, add the cooled oats mixture and 2½ cups of the flour. Beat with an electric mixer 2 minutes or at least 200 strokes by hand. Mix in the nuts. Gradually add more flour, as much as it takes to produce a dough which clings together and leaves the sides of the bowl.

Turn the dough out onto a floured board and knead until smooth and elastic, adding a little more flour if it remains too sticky to handle. Exercise restraint with the flour and expect the dough to be a little tacky because of the oats.

Put the dough into a buttered bowl, turn all around to coat or brush the top with melted butter. Cover with a towel and let rise until doubled in bulk.

Punch the dough down, turn out onto a lightly floured board, knead a few times to press out air bubbles, cut in half, cover and let rest about 10 minutes.

Shape the dough into smooth oblongs and place in two buttered, medium loaf pans. Brush the tops with melted butter. Cover with the towel and let rise again until almost doubled.

Preheat oven to 350°F. Bake 45 minutes, or until the bottoms sound hollow when tapped. Remove from pans and cool on a rack.

Makes two loaves.

CARROT BREAD

Invitingly flecked with orange, this loaf is one of the surest ways to get a carrot into some young mouths. It is not especially sweet and is therefore more suited to soup than tea.

Preheat the oven to 325°F.

In a mixing bowl beat the eggs until they are light and somewhat thickened. Beat in the maple syrup or honey, then the butter or oil and vanilla. Stir in the carrots, nuts and raisins, distributing evenly. Sift together the flour, baking powder, soda, cinnamon, ginger and salt. Add to the liquids and fold in until just mixed.

Pour the batter into a greased medium loaf pan and bake for 45-50 minutes, or until the top feels springy. Let it sit in the pan for about 10 minutes before removing to cool on a rack.

Makes one medium loaf.

2 eggs

½ cup maple syrup or ⅓ cup honey

½ cup melted sweet butter or light oil or a combination

1 teaspoon vanilla

1¼ cups grated or shredded raw carrot

¾ cup chopped nuts

½ cup gold raisins (optional)

1½ cups unbleached white flour

1½ teaspoons baking powder

½ teaspoon baking soda

1 teaspoon ground cinnamon

½ teaspoon ground ginger

½ teaspoon salt

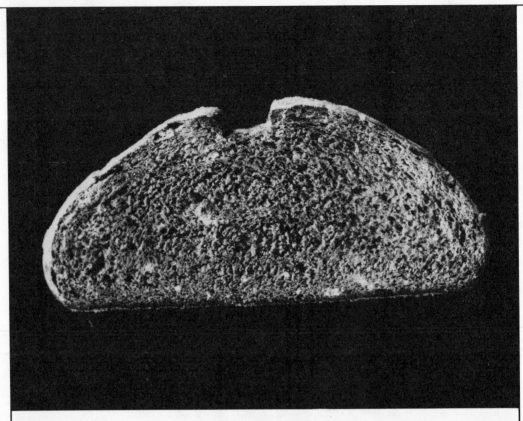

Pumpernickel.

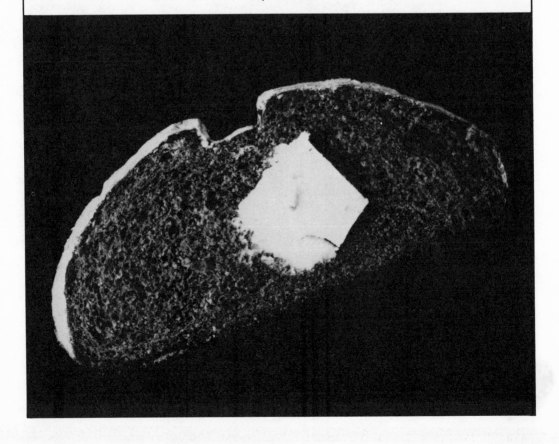

RAISIN PUMPERNICKEL

This closely textured loaf is a poem of dark grains, fragrant seeds, and sweet raisins. A favorite for informal suppers or elegant buffets.

In a large mixing bowl dissolve the yeast in the ½ cup warm water with the ½ teaspoon sugar or honey. When frothing, add the 2 cups water, butter, molasses, salt, fennel, caraway, 2 cups of the white flour, and 2 cups whole wheat flour. Beat very thoroughly, 2 minutes with an electric mixer or at least 200 strokes by hand. Sprinkle in the cornmeal slowly, stirring constantly.

Mix in the raisins, being sure they are evenly distributed and don't stick together. With a wooden spoon beat in the rye flour and enough more white to make a dough that clings together and leaves the sides of the bowl.

Turn the dough out onto a floured board and knead until smooth and elastic, sprinkling with a little more white flour if you must. Avoid adding too much flour or you will have a dry loaf. Despite all efforts this dough will remain obstinately sticky, but this will disappear after the first rise. When it reaches a state of elasticity, even though it still doesn't want to let go of your fingers, you can stop kneading.

Place the dough in a buttered bowl, turn to coat or brush the top with melted butter, cover with a damp towel and let rise until double in volume.

Punch the dough down. Unless you are in a rush, allow it to rise a second time in the bowl, again covered. It will rise faster this time. When it has doubled, punch the dough down again, turn out onto a lightly floured board, knead a few times, cut in half, cover and let rest for 10 to 15 minutes.

Butter a large baking sheet or two smaller ones. Dust with cornmeal. Shape the dough into long ovals (fatter than French breads). Place on the baking sheet(s) and slash crosswise several times on the tops with a sharp knife, about ¼-inch deep. Brush with melted butter, cover and let rise again until almost doubled.

Preheat the oven to 350°F. Bake 40 to 45 minutes, or until the bottoms sound hollow when tapped.

If you wish a glossy crust, about 10 minutes before you expect the bread to be done brush the surfaces with a glaze of egg white beaten with a tablespoon water.

Lift loaves to a rack to cool.

Makes two oval loaves.

½ cup warm water

2 tablespoons dry yeast

½ teaspoon sugar or honey

2 cups warm water

2 tablespoons soft sweet butter or light oil

½ cup unsulphured molasses

2 teaspoons salt

1 teaspoon fennel seed

1 teaspoon caraway seed

2½ cups unbleached white flour, approximately

2 cups whole wheat flour, preferably stone-ground

½ cup cornmeal, preferably stone-ground

1½ cups raisins (preferably gold)

2 cups rye flour, preferably stone-ground

SPICY STEAMED BROWN BREAD

½ cup hot water

1¼ cups bread crumbs, preferably made from stale homemade bread (grate on a large-holed grater or grind in a food processor)

⅓ cup white flour

2 teaspoons baking soda

1 teaspoon salt

¼ teaspoon allspice

¼ teaspoon white pepper

¼ teaspoon mace

1 cup rye flour, preferably stone-ground

¾ cup cornmeal preferably stone-ground

1 cup currants

½ cup unsulphured molasses

¼ cup honey

1 cup buttermilk or sour milk

4 tablespoons melted sweet butter

Pour the hot water over the bread crumbs and let sit a bit.

Sift together the white flour, baking soda, salt, allspice, white pepper and mace. Add the rye flour and cornmeal and stir well to mix. Toss in the currants.

In a large bowl beat together the molasses, honey, buttermilk and butter. Mix in the softened bread crumbs.

Add the flour mixture and blend gently but thoroughly with a rubber spatula or wooden spoon.

Divide the batter between two buttered 1-lb. coffee cans. Cover the tops with foil and secure tightly around the cans with string or tape. Place the cans on a trivet or cake rack in a large pot of boiling water, which should reach halfway up the sides of the cans. Cover the pot tightly and let the water simmer (not boil) for 3 hours.

Remove the cans and their covers and put them in a 300°F. oven for about 10 minutes to dry out slightly. Then let them sit on a rack for another 5 minutes or so before sliding the loaves out of their cans. Allow them to finish cooling on the rack if not eating immediately.

Makes two round loaves.

Do not use bread machine even
maybe if halfed for dough

CRACKED WHEAT BREAD

A tender, crunchy, chewy, and light, though coarsely grained, loaf. Satisfying and possibly habit-forming.

Put the cracked wheat in a bowl and pour the boiling water over it. Let it stand for an hour (or until you are ready to proceed). In a saucepan heat the buttermilk to a simmer, add the molasses, honey, butter and salt. Stir to mix; cool to lukewarm.

In a large mixing bowl dissolve the yeast in the warm water with half-teaspoon sugar or honey. When it is frothing, add the cooled buttermilk mixture and 2 cups of the white flour. Beat thoroughly, 2 minutes with an electric mixer or 200 strokes by hand. Stir in the cracked wheat.

Gradually add the whole wheat flour and enough additional white flour to make a dough that pulls together and leaves the sides of the bowl. Turn the dough out onto a floured surface and knead, adding a little more flour if the dough remains too sticky to work.

Be patient: this dough will cling to your fingers almost indefinitely; if it doesn't, you have probably added too much flour. When it becomes nicely resilient, even if still somewhat tacky, you can stop kneading. Place the dough in a buttered bowl, turn all around to coat or brush the top with melted butter. Cover and let rise again until doubled in bulk. Punch the dough down, turn out onto a lightly floured surface, knead a few times. Cover and let rest for about 10 minutes.

Cut the dough into 2 or 3 pieces, shape into oblongs and place in 2 quite large buttered loaf pans (or casseroles) or 3 medium loaf pans. Brush the tops with melted butter, cover and let rise again until doubled or almost doubled. Preheat the oven to 350°F. Bake about 45 minutes for large loaves, 35 minutes for medium, or until the bottoms sound hollow when tapped. If you like a glossy crust, about 10 minutes before you expect the loaves to be done brush them with an egg beaten with 2 tablespoons milk or water. Remove from pans to cool on a rack.

Slice off an end as soon as you can handle the bread without burning your fingers. Let a pat of butter melt on it and tear in half to share with a friend. In this way an entire loaf has been known to disappear before it has cooled.

Makes 2 large or 3 medium loaves.

¾ cup cracked wheat or bulgur

1½ cups boiling water

1 cup buttermilk or sour milk

¼ cup unsulphured molasses

2 tablespoons honey

¼ cup sweet butter (½ stick) or light oil

2 teaspoons salt

1½ tablespoons dry yeast

¼ cup warm water

½ teaspoon sugar or honey

3 cups unbleached white flour, approximately

2 cups whole wheat flour, approximately, preferably stone-ground

Egg for glaze (optional)

BRAN BATTER BREAD

1½ cups milk

2 tablespoons sweet butter

½ cup honey

2 teaspoons salt

2 tablespoons dry yeast

½ teaspoon sugar or honey

½ cup warm water

2 eggs

6 cups unbleached white flour, approximately

½ cup bran flakes (not bran cereal)

⅔ cup chopped pecans or walnuts

⅔ cup raisins

In a saucepan scald the milk; add the butter, honey and salt and let it sit until lukewarm.

In a large bowl dissolve the yeast and ½ teaspoon sugar or honey in the ½ cup water. When this is bubbly, add the eggs and the cooled milk mixture and beat. Add about 3 cups flour and beat very thoroughly, 5 to 10 minutes. Mix in the bran flakes, nuts and raisins. Add about 3 cups more flour, beating or stirring until the dough holds together and leaves the sides of the bowl.

Let the dough rise in its bowl, covered with a towel, until it has doubled in size. If you wish a finer texture, stir it down and let the dough rise again in the bowl.

Stir the dough down and divide equally between two large (about 9 × 5-inches) buttered loaf pans. Push it into the corners and try to smooth out the top surface with spoon or hands. Let the dough rise again, covered, until it reaches the tops of the pans.

Preheat the oven to 350°F. Bake 30 minutes, then take the loaves from their pans and put them on the oven rack for an additional 5 minutes, or until they test done.

Makes two large loaves.

JAMAICAN GINGERBREAD

Dark and emphatically gingery.

3 cups unbleached white flour

2½ teaspoons baking powder

½ teaspoon baking soda

½ teaspoon salt

1 teaspoon allspice

2 eggs

½ cup melted sweet butter, or part butter and part light oil

½ cup unsulphured molasses

1 cup evaporated milk or half and half

3 tablespoons grated fresh ginger root (if unavailable, use 1 tablespoon ground ginger sifted with the flour)

½ cup chopped crystallized ginger

1 cup chopped nuts (optional)

Preheat oven to 350°F.

Sift together the flour, baking powder, soda, salt and allspice. In a large bowl beat the eggs until light and slightly thick. Add the melted butter, molasses and evaporated milk and beat again. Stir in the ginger root, crystallized ginger and nuts (if using). Fold in the flour mixture, blending with a spatula until just incorporated.

Pour batter into a buttered large loaf pan and bake 50 minutes or until the top feels springy. Let rest in the pan about 10 minutes before removing to a rack.

Slice thinly and serve with sweet butter or whipped cream cheese.

Makes one large loaf.

SQUASH ROLLS

An ordinary vegetable becomes an extraordinary treat. This delicious dish can be made of pumpkin, too, should you have one not defaced during the Halloween season.

In a saucepan scald the milk. Add the maple syrup, butter, salt and squash, stirring to mix well. Let sit until lukewarm.

In a large bowl dissolve the yeast in the warm water with the ½ teaspoon sugar or honey. When it is bubbly, add the cooled milk-squash mixture, eggs, orange peel and 2½ cups of the flour. Beat with an electric mixer 2 minutes or at least 200 strokes by hand. Gradually add enough more flour to make a dough that pulls away from the sides of the bowl and is stiff enough to knead.

Turn the dough out onto a floured board and knead until smooth and elastic, sprinkling with a little more flour if it remains sticky.

Put the dough into a buttered bowl, turn to coat all sides or brush the top with melted butter. Cover and let rise until doubled in bulk.

Punch the dough down, turn out onto a floured board and knead a few times to press out air bubbles. Cut into pieces about the size of eggs, cover and let rest for 10 to 15 minutes. Form into rolls of whatever shape you wish (the easiest is to make balls and put in buttered muffin tins). Brush the tops with melted butter and let rise, lightly covered, until not quite double in size.

Preheat the oven to 375°F. Bake 15 minutes, or until done. Break one open to test. Do not overbake. Serve hot, or, if you plan to save them until the next meal or freeze, bake for a slightly shorter time, cool on a rack and re-heat.

Makes about two dozen rolls.

1 cup milk

¼ cup maple syrup or honey

4 tablespoons sweet butter or light oil

2 teaspoons salt

1 cup cooked winter squash (fresh or frozen). You may also use pumpkin, fresh or canned

1½ tablespoons dry yeast

¼ cup warm water

½ teaspoon sugar or honey

2 eggs

1 teaspoon grated orange peel

6½ cups unbleached white flour, approximately

PARATHAS

Parathas are fried on a griddle-like chappatis-but are more opulent: softer, flakier and buttery. Clarified butter is the **sine qua non.**

1 cup unbleached white flour

1½ teaspoons salt

3 cups whole wheat flour, preferably stone-ground

5 tablespoons chilled clarified butter*

1 cup cold water, approximately, or part water and part milk, or part water and part yogurt

½ cup melted clarified butter

*To clarify butter: Melt slowly in a saucepan. Pour off the clear yellow liquid, discard the white residue.

In a large bowl sift together the white flour and salt. Stir in the whole wheat flour, mixing well with a fork. Add the cold butter in pieces and cut it in with a pastry blender or two knives until the mixture is coarsely textured. Add enough water or other liquid to make a dough that holds together and is soft but manageable. Turn the dough out onto a lightly floured board and knead thoroughly for 5 to 10 minutes. Wrap the dough in a damp kitchen towel and let it rest for an hour or so, or chill overnight in the refrigerator.

When ready to cook, cut the dough into 16-18 equal pieces. On a lightly floured board, with a floured rolling pin, roll out each piece into a thin round. Brush the round with melted clarified butter. Fold it in half. Brush the half-moon-shaped dough with clarified butter. Fold it in half again so you now have a piece one-quarter the size of the original round. Re-flour your rolling pin and roll out the triangle very thin, keeping a semblance of its triangle shape if possible.

Fry the parathas on a preheated griddle over moderately high heat, brushing the griddle with clarified butter before each one. Fry until nicely browned on each side. While the bottom is browning, brush the top with more clarified butter in preparation for its turn on the griddle. The browning will be spotty rather than even, but you'll be able to tell if it is done by biting into one.

Serve the parathas hot. Of course they are perfect for Indian or other Eastern meals but also are fine with much American fare; for instance, a simple bowl of homemade soup. They may be kept warm in a low oven, with paper towels between them, until serving time.

Makes 16-18.

December

CARROT APRICOT STEAMED BREAD

An unusual, refreshingly tart bread, to clear your palate after days of eggnog and bonbons.

2 cups unbleached white flour

2 teaspoons baking powder

1 teaspoon salt

1 cup whole wheat flour, preferably stone-ground

2 eggs

⅔ cup honey

1⅓ cups milk

4 tablespoons melted sweet butter

1 teaspoon grated orange rind

1 cup grated raw carrots

1 cup chopped apricots

Sift together the white flour, baking powder and salt. Add the whole wheat flour and mix well with a fork.

In a large bowl beat the eggs until they are light and thick. Add the honey, milk, butter and grated orange rind, beating to mix. Stir in the grated carrot and apricots. Add the flour mixture and blend thoroughly but gently with a rubber spatula or wooden spoon.

Divide the batter between two buttered 1-lb. coffee cans. Cover the tops with foil and secure it tightly around the cans with string or tape. Place the cans on a trivet or cake rack in a large pot of boiling water, which should reach halfway up the cans. Cover the pot tightly and let the water simmer (not boil) for 3 hours. Remove the covers and place the cans in a 300°F. oven for about 10 minutes to dry out slightly. Then let them sit on a rack for another 5 minutes or so before sliding the breads out of their cans. Allow them to finish cooling on the rack if not eating immediately.

Makes two round loaves.

HUTZELBROT
(German Fruit and Nut Bread)

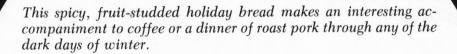

This spicy, fruit-studded holiday bread makes an interesting accompaniment to coffee or a dinner of roast pork through any of the dark days of winter.

If any of the dried fruit is hard, simmer it in water to cover about 10 minutes and let sit a half-hour. If it is reasonably soft this is not necessary. Drain well any of the fruit which you have cooked. Chop all the fruit (except raisins) and toss fruit, including raisins with ¼ cup flour.

In a large mixing bowl combine the yeast, warm water and ½ teaspoon sugar or honey. Let sit until bubbling. Add 1 cup liquid (either that in which fruit is cooked, or juice); the liquid may be warm but not hot. Add the anise seed, cinnamon, salt, lemon peel, cloves, honey and melted butter. Beat well to mix. Add 2½ cups of the flour and beat at least 200 strokes by hand or 2 minutes with an electric mixer. Stir in the nuts. Gradually add more flour until the dough holds together and leaves the sides of the bowl. Turn it out onto a floured board and knead until smooth and elastic, adding a little more flour as necessary but trying to keep a soft dough. Put the dough into a buttered bowl, turn to coat all sides or brush the top with melted butter. Cover with a towel and let rise until doubled in bulk.

Punch the dough down, turn out onto a lightly floured board, knead a few times and press the dough out into a large oval with your hands. Sprinkle the surface with some of the chopped fruit. Fold the dough in half and press out again into a large oval. Sprinkle with more fruit. Repeat this process until all the fruit has been incorporated. Don't be surprised if the pressing becomes a bit harder each time. Ignore any flour that is left in the bottom of the fruit bowl.

Cut the dough in half with a sharp knife, cover with the towel and let rest 10 to 15 minutes. With your hands form each piece of dough into an oblong, something like a meatloaf. Place on buttered cookie sheets and brush the tops with melted butter (if you put them both on one sheet be sure there is room in all directions for expansion). Cover with a light cloth and let rise until not quite doubled.

Preheat the oven to 350°F. Bake loaves 40 to 45 minutes, or until bottoms sound hollow when thumped. Cool on a rack.

When cool, glaze with an icing of confectioners' sugar and milk, if you wish, and decorate with blanched almond halves and candied cherries.

1 cup pitted prunes

1 cup dried peaches, pears or apricots

½ cup dried figs

Note: if above ingredients are unavailable, use 2½ cups mixed dried fruit

½ cup raisins

¼ cup unbleached white flour

½ cup warm water

1½ tablespoons dry yeast

½ teaspoon sugar or honey

1 cup liquid from cooking fruit or fruit juice, such as orange, pineapple, or apricot nectar

1 teaspoon anise seed

1 teaspoon cinnamon

1 teaspoon salt

1 teaspoon grated lemon or orange peel

½ teaspoon ground cloves

¼ cup honey

½ cup melted butter (1 stick)

5 cups unbleached white flour, approximately

½ cup chopped walnuts

½ cup sliced almonds

Confectioners' sugar, blanched almond halves, candied cherries (optional)

Greek Christmas bread.

CHRISTOPSOMO (Greek Christmas Bread)

Fragrant, tender and rich, this spectacular bread is sumptuous with tea or coffee, either warm or cool. It is so pretty you may feel it should be preserved in varnish, but do give in to your baser instincts and eat it. As a friend said, revel and grovel.

In a saucepan scald the milk. Add the butter, honey and salt; stir and let sit until lukewarm.

In a large mixing bowl combine the yeast, warm water and ½ teaspoon sugar or honey. Wait until this mixture is foaming, then add the cooled milk, eggs and anise. Beat thoroughly. Add 3 cups of the flour and beat at least 200 strokes by hand or 2 minutes with an electric mixer. Gradually add more flour until the dough clings together in the center of the bowl.

Turn the dough out onto a floured board and knead until smooth and elastic, adding a little more flour if necessary. This should be an easy dough to knead and should lose its stickiness early, although it will feel somewhat oily because of the butter.

Place the dough in a buttered bowl, turn to grease the top or brush with melted butter, cover with a cloth and let rise until doubled in bulk.

Punch the dough down, turn out onto a lightly floured board, knead a few times to press out air bubbles, and cut off two pieces of dough, each the size of a small apple. Cover the dough and pieces with a towel and let rest about 10 minutes.

Shape the large hunk of dough into a smooth ball (press out with hands into a flattened round, tuck all the edges underneath and seal together at center bottom, coax the dough with your hands into a nice round ball, then press again to flatten slightly; it should still swell in the middle). Place on a *large*, buttered cookie sheet or jelly roll pan.

Roll out each small piece of dough with your palms into a thin rope about half again as long as the diameter of your flattened ball. Try to make the rope even in thickness. Use a sharp knife to split the rope in half for 4 inches on each end. Repeat with the other rope.

Carefully place one of the ropes across the large loaf so that it intersects it across the middle, leaving equal amounts of overhang on either end. Place the second rope at right angles to the first one so that they form a cross on top of the dough. Curl each split end away from the center to make a small circle, which lies on the slope of the large loaf. Now the end of each rope will look like an anchor. It will help if the anchors are formed high enough up on the loaf so that they don't collapse down over the sides during baking. Tack each curlique in place with toothpicks or pieces of raw spaghetti. Brush the dough with melted butter and let rise, covered with a light cloth, until almost doubled in size.

Preheat the oven to 350°F. Brush the entire bread with an egg white beaten with a tablespoon of water. Place a walnut or pecan half in the hollow of each curlique (two for each "anchor") and at the center of the cross. Press gently so they will adhere.

Bake 40-50 minutes. Raise loaf carefully with a pancake turner to tap bottom for doneness, or plunge a cake tester into the side. Cool on a rack. Cut in wedges or slices.

Makes 1 large loaf.

1 cup milk
½ cup sweet butter (1 stick)
½ cup honey
1½ teaspoons salt
2 tablespoons dry yeast
½ cup warm water
½ teaspoon sugar or honey
4 eggs
1 teaspoon anise seed, bruised with the back of a spoon (or 1½ teaspoons if you prefer a more definite flavor)
6-7 cups unbleached white flour
9 perfect walnut or pecan halves
1 egg white for glaze

SPICE MUFFINS

Very good

1 cup unbleached white flour

1 cup rye flour, preferably stone-ground

2 teaspoons baking powder

½ teaspoon baking soda

½ teaspoon salt

½ teaspoon white pepper

½ teaspoon nutmeg

¾ teaspoon cinnamon

¼ teaspoon ground ginger

¼ teaspoon ground cloves

½ cup currants or raisins

2 eggs

⅓ cup maple syrup or honey

⅔ cup buttermilk or sour milk

4 tablespoons melted sweet butter

Preheat the oven to 400°F. Sift together the white and rye flour, baking powder, soda, salt, pepper and spices. Toss in the currants or raisins.

In another bowl beat the eggs until they are light in color and slightly thickened. Add the maple syrup or honey, buttermilk and butter and beat well. Stir in the flour mixture with a rubber spatula or wooden spoon until the flour is almost incorporated and the batter is still rough and lumpy.

Spoon the batter into buttered muffin tins, filling each ⅔ full. Bake 18-20 minutes. Break one apart to test for doneness.

Makes 12-14 muffins.

NORWEGIAN APPLE PANCAKES

These crepes are festive for brunch or dessert.

First start the filling. Saute the apples in the butter over low heat, adding the cinnamon and lemon rind. When the apples are beginning to get soft, add the currant jelly and stir until it melts. Keep warm.

Beat the eggs and egg yolk until they are light in color and thickened. Add the milk, vanilla, cardamon, salt and melted butter and beat well. Sift in the flour and beat to mix. This will make a thin batter.

Preheat to medium hot and lightly grease an 8- or 9-inch skillet, preferably one with sloping sides (which will make the turning easier). Pour in about ¼ cup of the batter. When brown on the bottom, turn and cook till brown and crisp on the other side. You will (we trust) become adept at sliding an egg turner under a corner of the pancake, maneuvering it into the approximate middle and flipping the cake over with one deft motion.

Remove the pancake, put 2 to 3 tablespoons of apple filling in the center, fold one edge over and then the other to cover the filling, then turn the whole rolled pancake over so the seam is down. Sprinkle with sugar and slivered almonds. Serve at once or keep warm on a platter in a low oven until the rest are done. It probably will not be necessary to grease the skillet for subsequent pancakes, but if the cakes stick, brush on a little more oil with a pastry brush.

This quantity makes about 14 pancakes. You should probably serve two per person for dessert; one might suffice for brunch if there are other dishes.

Apple filling:
- 4 cups very thinly sliced peeled apples
- 4 tablespoons butter
- ¼ teaspoon cinnamon
- 1 teaspoon grated lemon peel
- 5 tablespoons currant jelly

Batter:
- 2 eggs and 1 egg yolk
- 1½ cups milk
- ¼ teaspoon vanilla
- ⅛ teaspoon ground cardamon
- ⅛ teaspoon salt
- ¼ cup melted sweet butter
- 1 cup unbleached white flour

Topping:
- granulated sugar
- slivered almonds

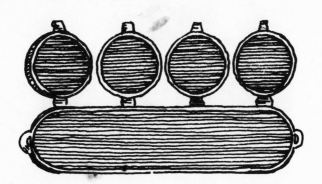

Saffron braid.

SAFFRON BRAID

For appetites that may have become jaded with ordinary, everyday delicious homemade bread, here is something a little different. It is shapely, golden in color and spiked by the exotic flavor of saffron. Saffron is usually packed in tiny quantities and is expensive. It recalls the days when spices were not universally available in little glass jars but were something rare and precious.

In a large mixing bowl pour the boiling orange juice or water over the saffron threads and let steep. Scald the milk in a saucepan. Add the butter, honey and salt. Stir to melt and let sit until lukewarm. Meanwhile, test the saffron water with your finger or a thermometer. When it has cooled to warm (not over 110°F.) add the yeast with the ½ teaspoon sugar or honey. Stir and wait until the yeast is bubbly. Add the cooled milk mixture and eggs and beat well. Add 3 cups of the flour and beat at least 200 strokes by hand or 2 minutes with an electric mixer. Stir in the raisins. Gradually add the remaining flour, or enough to make a dough too stiff to beat that pulls away from the sides of the bowl. Turn the dough out onto a floured board and knead until smooth and elastic, adding a little more flour as necessary. Try to keep the dough on the soft side.

Place the dough in a buttered bowl, turn to coat all sides or brush the top with melted butter. Cover with a towel and let rise until doubled in bulk.

Punch the dough down, turn out onto a lightly floured board, knead a few times and, with a sharp knife, cut in half. Cut each half into three equal pieces, cover, and let rest about 10 minutes.

Butter two large loaf pans. Take the pieces of dough one at a time, leaving the rest wrapped in the towel, and roll them out with your palms into a rope that is more or less uniformly thick and about half again as long as your loaf pan. Braid three of the ropes, pinching the ends together to seal and tucking them under. Repeat with the other three ropes. With your hands, gently compress or stretch the braid to make it the same length as your loaf pan. Place the braids carefully in their pans, trying not to squash any of the strands in the process. Don't worry if they're a little misshapen; they will improve as they rise.

Brush the tops of the braids with melted butter, making sure it gets into the creases and crannies. Cover with a light cloth and let rise until not quite double.

Preheat the oven to 375°F. Bake about 35 minutes or until the bottoms of the loaves sound hollow when tapped. About 10 minutes before you expect the loaves to be done, remove from the oven and brush the tops with a glaze of whole egg beaten with 2 tablespoons milk or water. Alternatively, you can make free-form braids on baking sheets, in which case the baking time will be slightly less. Cool on racks.

Makes two large braids.

¾ cup boiling orange juice or water
¾ teaspoon saffron threads (if you can't find the threads, use ¼ teaspoon powdered saffron)
1½ cups milk
½ cup honey
½ cup sweet butter (1 stick)
1½ teaspoons salt
1½ tablespoons dry yeast
½ teaspoon sugar or honey
1 egg
6–7 cups unbleached white flour
½–1 cup gold raisins
Egg for glaze

NORTH CAROLINA SPICY CHEESE BISCUITS

These crisp wafers, popular since colonial times, are still held in great favor. Because of the seasoning, they are served for hors d'oeuvres or snacks, not with meals. They are especially popular around Christmas and a tin of them makes a splendid gift. Warning: they are fairly addictive and unfairly fattening.

1 cup unbleached white flour

1 teaspoon salt

½ cup sweet butter (1 stick), softened

2 cups grated sharp cheddar cheese

Tabasco to taste (some like it hot, some hotter; ¼ teaspoon is perceptible, ½ teaspoon, emphatic)

Pecan halves (about 100)

Sift together the flour and salt. Blend into the butter and cheese with an electric mixer or wooden spoon. Add the tabasco and mix well. Divide the dough into two balls and roll each with your palms on a lightly floured board into a cylinder about 1- to 1½-inch thick. Wrap in wax paper and chill overnight, or from morning till night.

Unwrap the rolls and slice thinly with a sharp knife. Place the rounds on ungreased baking sheets and press a pecan half into the top of each one.

Bake in a 350°F. oven for 10 to 15 minutes, depending on thickness. This makes at least 100 small wafers, which sounds like an excess. They freeze extremely well and thaw quickly. They also keep well in a tightly covered tin. Especially one with a lock and key.

CRANBERRY FRITTERS

These are pleasantly tart and would be a fine accompaniment to winter meals.

2 cups raw cranberries

2 eggs

6 tablespoons honey

2 tablespoons melted sweet butter

2 teaspoons grated orange peel

1¼ cups unbleached white flour

¼ teaspoon salt

2 teaspoons baking powder

Confectioners' sugar

Chop the cranberries coarsely and cook in water to cover until just soft. Drain well in a colander and then on paper towels. Beat the eggs until light and slightly thickened. Add the honey and beat, then the melted butter and orange rind and beat to mix. Stir in the cranberries. Sift together the flour, salt and baking powder. Add to the cranberry mixture and blend gently.

Drop the batter from a teaspoon into deep fat which has been preheated to between 350° and 365°F. Use a candy thermometer and leave it in the pot so you can maintain the right temperature. Fry the fritters, a few at a time, until golden brown on both sides, which will probably take 3 to 4 minutes. Remove with a slotted spoon and drain on paper towels. Break open one of the first ones to check for proper doneness; they should be slightly moist but not runny. Sift confectioners' sugar over the fritters, if desired, and serve while still warm. (They can be held in a slow oven for a while if necessary.)

This makes about 18.

DUTCH DOUGHNUTS

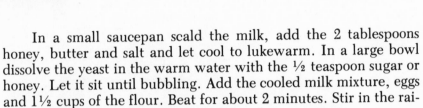

These spicy yeast doughnuts contain raisins and apples and are something special.

In a small saucepan scald the milk, add the 2 tablespoons honey, butter and salt and let cool to lukewarm. In a large bowl dissolve the yeast in the warm water with the ½ teaspoon sugar or honey. Let it sit until bubbling. Add the cooled milk mixture, eggs and 1½ cups of the flour. Beat for about 2 minutes. Stir in the raisins, apples, lemon peel, orange peel and cinnamon.

Gradually add about 1½ cups more flour, or enough to make a dough that pulls away from the sides of the bowl and is too stiff to beat. Turn the dough out onto a lightly floured board and knead until smooth and elastic, sprinkling with a little more flour only if necessary. Seek to maintain a soft dough.

Place the dough in a buttered bowl and turn to coat all sides, or brush the top with melted butter. Cover with a kitchen towel and let rise until doubled in bulk.

Punch the dough down, turn it out onto the lightly floured board and knead a few times to press out air bubbles. With a knife cut the dough into 32 equal pieces (cut the whole dough in half, then each half in half, each quarter in half, and so on). If the pieces seem sticky on their cut sides, roll them lightly on the floured board. Cover them and let rest for 10 to 15 minutes.

Form each little piece of dough into a ball. The easiest way to do this is to press the piece flat with your palm, then tuck all the edges under and pinch them together, with your hands gently coaxing the dough into a sphere. You'll have a pinched seam on the bottom but the top will be nice and smooth. Let the balls rise on lightly floured baking sheets, or the board, covered with a thin kitchen towel, until they are almost but not quite double in size.

Meanwhile heat deep fat in a large pot to 375°F. Use a candy thermometer and leave it in the pot to help you keep the heat steady. One at a time lift the balls very gently onto a spatula and ease them into the hot fat. Cook only a few at a time. Fry until crisp and brown on both sides, about 4 minutes in all.

Remove with a slotted spoon and drain on paper towels. Break open one of the first ones to test for proper doneness; they should be moist on the inside but not doughy. While they are still hot and the next batch is frying, roll each doughnut in a bowl of cinnamon sugar until it is coated on all sides. Since the doughnuts are still too hot to hold, do this with the aid of a spoon. These doughnuts are best while hot but still good when cooled. Makes 32 doughnuts.

Cinnamon sugar: ½ cup sugar and 2 to 3 teaspoons cinnamon, as you desire. Mix well with a fork.

½ cup milk

2 tablespoons honey

1 tablespoon sweet butter

¼ teaspoon salt

¼ cup warm water

1 tablespoon dry yeast

½ teaspoon sugar or honey

2 eggs

3 cups unbleached white flour, approximately

¾ cup gold raisins

¾ cup minced peeled tart apples

1 teaspoon grated lemon peel

1 teaspoon grated orange peel

½ teaspoon cinnamon

Journeymen bakers form breads from huge lump of dough at Moravian Bakery.

MORAVIAN LOVE FEAST BUNS

A memory of adolescence in a Moravian school is the Love Feast, a religious service featuring music, candles and food which takes place on days of celebration in the Church calendar. The connection with Communion seems obvious, but here the breaking of bread is not as symbolic of the union with Christ as of the earthly fellowship of people with each other. Men of the church pass trays of coffee, served in heavy ceramic mugs that keep it scalding hot for a long time. Steeped with sugar and cream, it is almost the best coffee one could imagine. Women stop at each pew with huge baskets of Love Feast Buns, large puffy sweet rolls of ineffable goodness. The combination of coffee and bread, music, candles (for everyone receives a beeswax candle nestled in a red paper frill) and human companionship make the name Love Feast seem exactly right.

Love Feast Buns are delectable warm from the oven, although at Love Feasts they are served at room temperature. If you aren't starting a Moravian congregation, serve them for breakfast, tea or coffee any time of the day.

In a large mixing bowl dissolve the yeast in ½ cup of the warm potato water with the ½ teaspoon sugar or honey. Let it sit until bubbling. Add the other ½ cup potato water, cup honey, eggs, salt, softened butter and shortening, mashed potatoes, mace and orange peel. Beat to combine well.

Add 3 cups of the flour and beat 2 minutes with an electric mixer or at least 200 strokes by hand. Gradually add 4 to 4½ cups more flour, or enough to make a dough that clings together and leaves the sides of the bowl.

Turn the dough out onto a floured board and knead until smooth and elastic, sprinkling with a little more flour if it remains too sticky. Be patient and expect the dough to be clingy because of the potatoes; try to keep it on the soft side. Put the dough into a buttered bowl, turn to coat all sides or brush the top with melted butter, cover with a towel and let rise until doubled in bulk.

Punch the dough down, turn it out onto a lightly floured board and knead a few times to press out air bubbles. Cut into 18 to 24 equal pieces (cut dough in half, cut each half in half, cut each quarter in half, etc.). Cover with the towel and let rest for 10 to 15 minutes. Shape each piece into a slightly flattened ball. Press a piece of dough flat with your palm, tuck all the edges under and pinch to seal them, leaving a smooth surface on top, and shape the dough between your hands until it is nicely round. Then press the top again to flatten just a bit. The traditional diameter is about 4 inches, but don't fret if yours are slightly smaller or larger than that.

Place the buns on baking sheets, leaving enough space between them to allow for swelling, and brush the tops with melted butter. If you don't have enough sheets, refrigerate part of the dough until ready to use. Cover with a light cloth and let rise again until not quite doubled in size. This can be done overnight in the refrigerator, in which case the cloth should be damp.

Preheat the oven to 425°F. Bake 10-15 minutes; you may tear one apart to test for doneness. After taking from the oven, brush the tops again with melted butter or cream. Cool on a rack, or eat while warm if you can think of a good reason.

2 tablespoons dry yeast

1 cup warm potato water

½ teaspoon sugar or honey

1 cup honey

2 eggs

2 teaspoons salt

¾ cup softened sweet butter, vegetable shortening, or lard, mixed in whatever proportion you desire

1 cup warm mashed potatoes

1 teaspoon mace

1 teaspoon grated orange peel (optional)

7-8 cups unbleached white flour

JULEBROD (Norwegian Christmas Wreath)

It is not necessary to make a wreath out of this bread, but if an extravagant holiday mood overtakes you, please do. It makes a beautiful present or centerpiece, or you can just leave it lying around to cut slices from as though you always did this sort of thing.

1¼ cups milk

⅓ cup honey

4 tablespoons sweet butter

1½ teaspoons salt

⅓ cup warm water

1½ tablespoons dry yeast

½ teaspoon sugar or honey

1 egg

1½ teaspoons ground cardamon

½ teaspoon mace

¼ teaspoon ground ginger

2 teaspoons grated orange peel

4-5 cups unbleached white flour

¾ cup mixed candied fruits and peels (optional)

½ cup gold raisins

Egg for glaze

In a saucepan scald the milk. Add the honey, butter and salt and let sit until lukewarm. In a large mixing bowl combine the yeast, warm water and ½ teaspoon sugar or honey. When bubbly add the cooled milk mixture, egg, cardamon, mace, ginger and orange peel. Beat well to mix. Add 2½ cups of the flour and beat at least 200 strokes by hand or 2 minutes with an electric mixer. Stir in the fruits and raisins. Gradually add more flour until the dough clings together and leaves the sides of the bowl. Turn out onto a floured board and knead until smooth and elastic, adding a little more flour as necessary but striving to keep a soft dough.

Put the dough in a buttered bowl, turn to coat all sides or brush top with melted butter, cover with a towel and let rise until doubled in bulk. Punch the dough down, turn out onto a lightly floured board, knead a few times to press out air bubbles and cut into three equal pieces. Cover and let rest about 10 minutes.

Work the pieces one at a time with your hands into long ropes. This takes some strenuous rolling with your palms. It also helps if you have a large surface to work on. The ropes should be skinny, of equal thickness, and about 30 to 36 inches long. This will seem quite long but they shrink a great deal when braided. Pinch the three ropes together at one end and braid them, not too tightly. When you've finished see if the braid will form a circle; if not, undo it and roll the ropes longer or braid them more loosely. Curl the braid into a circle on a buttered, large baking sheet (be sure there is room around the edges for expansion). Try to join the ends of the wreath together neatly by tucking them in and pinching together on the underneath side; don't worry as long as they are touching and no loose strand is poking out; they'll grow together.

It is helpful to put a jar in the middle of the wreath (butter it and the dough first) to maintain the hole in the center. You might also put a buttered springform collar around the outside to encourage the braid to rise up rather than out (it should be a bit larger than the wreath). Brush the wreath with melted butter, getting some into all the nooks and crannies. Cover with a light cloth and let rise until not quite double.

Preheat the oven to 350°F. Remove the jar and/or springform before baking. Bake about 30 minutes. Remove from oven and brush all over with a glaze of whole egg beaten with two tablespoons milk. Return to the oven for about 10 more minutes, or until a toothpick poked into the side comes out clean.

With two pancake turners carefully lift the wreath to a large rack to cool (or slide it off if your sheet has no sides). Drizzle with icing made of confectioners' sugar and milk and sprinkle with slivered almonds or, for a *trompe l'oeil* effect, decorate with sprigs of real holly and berries or candied red cherries, sliced in half.

If you don't want to bother with a wreath, simply make two round loaves and bake on cookie sheets until the bottoms sound hollow when tapped.

Makes one wreath or two loaves.

BOURBON BREAD

A celebratory loaf for a season of celebrations. It keeps well, it's nice to have on hand to serve drop-in guests and it makes a jolly gift with its slight whiff of sinfulness (only an illusion since the alcohol has evaporated). Bake it in a mold or Bundt pan and stick a sprig of holly in the middle with a plaid bow.

In a small bowl macerate the dates in the bourbon for a hour or several hours.

Preheat oven to 325°F. In a large mixing bowl beat the eggs until light and thick. Add the honey and beat. Beat in the butter, cream, vanilla and brandy. Stir in the raisins, pecans and dates with the bourbon (scrape out the bourbon bowl with a rubber spatula so you won't waste any). Mix to distribute evenly.

Sift together the flour, baking powder, soda, salt, nutmeg and cloves. Add to the liquids and fold in gently until just incorporated.

Pour the batter into a buttered mold, small Bundt pan or Kuglehopf pan, or large loaf pan. Bake 50 minutes or until the top feels springy and the edges are beginning to brown and shrink away from the pan. Don't overcook.

Let rest in the pan for about 10 minutes before unmolding onto a rack to cool. Store, wrapped in plastic wrap in a cool dry place (not the refrigerator). It will keep for about 5 days.

Makes one loaf.

1 cup unsweetened dates, chopped
⅓ cup bourbon
3 eggs
½ cup honey
¼ cup melted sweet butter
¼ cup heavy cream (or evaporated milk, half and half, or milk)
1 teaspoon vanilla
3 tablespoons brandy or cognac
½ cup raisins
1 cup chopped pecans
2 cups unbleached white flour
2½ teaspoons baking powder
½ teaspoon baking soda
½ teaspoon salt
½ teaspoon nutmeg
¼ teaspoon ground cloves

Index

Index